The Act of Prayer

Text copyright © John Birch 2014
The author asserts the moral right
to be identified as the author of this work

Published by
The Bible Reading Fellowship
15 The Chambers, Vineyard
Abingdon OX14 3FE
United Kingdom
Tel: +44 (0)1865 319700
Email: enquiries@brf.org.uk
Website: www.brf.org.uk
BRF is a Registered Charity

ISBN 978 1 84101 619 1
First published 2014
10 9 8 7 6 5 4 3 2 1 0

Scripture quotations are taken from The Holy Bible, New International Version
(Anglicised edition) copyright © 1979, 1984, 2011 by Biblica. Used by permission
of Hodder & Stoughton Publishers, an Hachette UK company. All rights reserved.
'NIV' is a registered trademark of Biblica. UK trademark number 1448790.

Cover photo: Spectral-Design/Thinkstock

A catalogue record for this book is available from the British Library

Printed and bound by CPI Group (UK) Ltd, Croydon CR0 4YY

The Act of Prayer

Praying through the lectionary

John Birch

Contents

Introduction

The Lord said to him: 'I have heard the prayer and plea you have made before me.'
1 KINGS 9:3 (NIV)

Prayers come in all shapes and colours. They reflect the faith and creativity of their authors and the influences that have been important in bringing them to the place where they are now. For myself, I have a fairly ecumenical background but am currently a Local Preacher within the Methodist Church, with an interest in the faith and prayer life of the early Christians in Britain and Ireland.

Within this collection you will find a variety of styles. The prayers are not all formatted in a traditional manner but they *are* written to be spoken, and, where lines are indented, the intention is a pause or emphasis. There's something to be said for slowing down our praying, so that the words can sink in.

However, within the context of our collective worship there are certain elements that it would seem right to include, in order that our prayers are not seen to be too narrow in their aspirations. These elements were at the very centre of the daily prayer life of the early church, and can be represented by the acronym ACT (Adoration, Confession and Thanksgiving).

The prayers follow the three-year lectionary cycle (the pattern of Bible readings followed by many denominations worldwide), and aim to reflect the readings for each Sunday in the year, along with a few extra days, such as Good Friday. Although there are some variations within denominations, I believe that all the main Sunday readings are covered. The cycle starts with the First Sunday of Advent because that is considered to be the beginning of the church year.

Year A

First Sunday of Advent

Sunday between 27 November and 3 December

ISAIAH 2:1–5; PSALM 122; ROMANS 13:11–14; MATTHEW 24:36–44

Opening prayer

I rejoiced with those who said,
  'Let us go to the house of
  the Lord.'

Father, Son and Spirit,
be with us in our unity,
our meeting and greeting,
our worship and fellowship,
our being and doing,
our reaching out to you.

I rejoiced with those who said,
  'Let us go to the house of
  the Lord.'

Adoration

God of hope and mystery,
  anticipation,
    preparation,
we wait for a kingdom
of this world and the next,
and a king
appearing when we least
  expect.
Heaven touches earth.
Footsteps of the divine
walk dusty roads
as once they did in Eden
  and a people,
searching for a saviour,
walk straight past
the stable.

Open our eyes and hearts
that this might be
an Advent of hope for the
  world,
where those who seek
will find
the Christ-child
born for them.

Confession

Forgive your people
who slumber
when there is need
for comfort
or peace to be shown,
who hesitate
where there is urgency
for your love
and grace to be known.
Forgive those of us
who are weary
of travelling,
tempted
to go our own way.
Forgive and restore
both faith and hope,
that by your grace
our lives might proclaim
the good news
of which we sing.

Thanksgiving

In this Advent of expectation
draw us together in unity,
that our praise and
   thanksgiving
might echo from these walls
and also through our lives.

Leader: God of Advent
All: Draw near, we pray.

In this Advent of expectation
draw us together in mission.
Let the gratitude in our hearts
be the song that we sing
and the melody of our lives.

Leader: God of Advent
All: Draw near, we pray.

In this Advent of expectation
draw us together in service,
that the path we follow
might lead from the stable
to a glimpse of eternity.

Leader: God of Advent
All: Draw near, we pray.

Second Sunday of Advent

Sunday between 4 and 10 December

ISAIAH 11:1–10; PSALM 72:1–7, 18–19; ROMANS 15:4–13; MATTHEW 3:1–12

Opening prayer

This is a time for preparation,
of walking toward Bethlehem,
making straight the path
that will lead others
into the presence of the divine.
We bring our gifts to you—
none greater
than the offering of our hearts
in worship and in praise.

Adoration

Spirit of wisdom,
rest upon us;
grant us
understanding
and an increase in our faith.

Spirit of knowledge,
rest upon us;
grant us
discernment
in decisions we must make.

Spirit of power,
rest upon us;
grant us
faithfulness
when we are spiritually weak.

Spirit of God,
present in Jesus,
Saviour,
rest upon us
this Advent time, we pray.

Confession

Advent God,
we journey with you
to Bethlehem's stable
and a newborn king,
ears attuned
to the song of angels,
eyes alert
for Bethlehem's star.

Forgive us
if on our journey
we are distracted
by the tempting offers
this world might bring.
Keep our hearts aflame
with the promise
of Advent,
and the birth
of our Saviour.

Thanksgiving

God of hope
who brought love into this
  world,
thank you for the love that
  dwells between us.

God of hope
who brought peace into this
  world,
thank you for the peace that
  dwells between us.

God of hope
who brought joy into this
  world,
thank you for the joy that
  dwells between us.

God of hope,
the rock upon which we stand,
thank you for the vision that
  unites us
this day and throughout this
  Advent time.

Third Sunday of Advent

Sunday between 11 December and 17 December

ISAIAH 35:1–10; PSALM 146:4–10; LUKE 1:46–55; JAMES 5:7–10; MATTHEW 11:2–11

Opening prayer

Advent God,
be with us in our journeying
to the stable and beyond.
Be with us in our meeting
and in our travelling together.
Be with us in our worship
and our praying together.
Be with us in our journeying
to the stable and beyond,
Advent God.

Adoration

We are blessed
if, knowing you as Lord,
we are obedient
to your word.

We are blessed
if, in our journeying,
we respond to your call
to follow.

We are blessed
as we draw together
in fellowship, prayer
and service.

Glorious God,
we are blessed,
we are blessed indeed.

Confession

God of wholeness,
healing and power,
forgive our reluctance
to open our hearts in prayer.
In the presence of Jesus
the blind received their sight,
lepers were healed,
the lame threw down their
  crutches
and leapt for joy;
good news was preached
to all who would hear.

We come to you
afraid to ask too much,
doubting your love and power.
Grant us courage in our
  prayers,
and the knowledge
that nothing,
absolutely nothing,
is impossible for you.

Thanksgiving

For the faithfulness
of your servant Mary
we give you thanks.
For saints of every age
who, when called,
have simply obeyed—
whether shepherd
or scholar,
faced by opposition
or praise,
asked to give
from their riches
or poverty—
we give you thanks.

In your eyes all are blessed.
May we count ourselves
among that number,
willing to hear your call,
our lives dedicated in service
to our Saviour and King.

Fourth Sunday of Advent

Sunday between 18 December and 24 December

ISAIAH 7:10–16; PSALM 80:1–7, 17–19; ROMANS 1:1–7; MATTHEW 1:18–25

Opening prayer

God of signs and wonders,
star and angels,
heaven touching earth
and the divine
entering human flesh,
be the peace among us
and the hope within us,
that we might become
your holy people
in this and every place
where you might take us.

Adoration

Immanuel,
God with us,
the eternal mystery
of the divine
about to touch this earth
in vulnerability and love,
through the humble witness
and patient obedience
of your servants Mary and
  Joseph.
What glorious news to share!

Immanuel,
God with us
as we gather together
in worship,
preparing to celebrate
the Saviour's birth
and once again to journey
spiritually to a stable,
with our grateful offerings of
  praise.
What glorious news to share!

Confession

Restore us, O Lord, we pray;
bring us back to that place
where we first met,
as shepherds to the stable
hearing angels sing
or wise men looking for signs
of a coming king.
Bring us back to that place
where our love was fresh,
not embarrassed
to express itself in praise
to the one who sets us free.
Bring us back to that place
and restore us, O Lord,
  we pray.

Thanksgiving

This Advent time
we remember Mary and
  Joseph,
giving thanks for their
  faithfulness,
courage and obedience,
stepping out into the unknown
in the strength of your Spirit,
playing their part
in the fulfilment of your plan
to bring a prodigal people
  home again.

May their example
be the pattern of our lives,
and when we hear your gentle
  whisper
grant us courage
to step out on our journey
  with you.

Year A

Christmas Day

ISAIAH 52:7–10; PSALM 98; HEBREWS 1:1–4 [5–12]; JOHN 1:1–14

Opening prayer

Saving God, who walked this
  earth
in Eden and by Galilee,
we praise you for your
  everlasting love,
enduring patience
and the greatest gift of all,
the possibility of salvation
through Jesus Christ our Lord.

Adoration

From the very beginning was
your Word
  which spoke this world into
  being,
your Word
  which thunders from the
  skies,
your Word
  which flows like mountain
  streams,
your Word
  which whispers in morning
  breeze,
your Word
  revealed through kings and
  prophets,
your Word
  revealed through angels'
  praise,
your Word
  revealed in humble service,
your Word
  revealed through a tiny child,
your Word
  alive from the beginning of all
  things
and to eternity.

Confession

You gave your all to the world
in the bleakness of that stable.
Love was born that day,
  pure love,
    undiluted,
poured out for all
who call on your name.

Such grace,
  undeserved,
demands our response.
Forgive our ingratitude
for a gift so freely given.
Draw us to your Word,
as the shepherds were drawn
  to the stable,
bringing our offering
of lives and love.
Give us a new song to sing
that will resonate
throughout this world
and the next.

Thanksgiving

Shout for joy,
the whole earth
and everything within.
Rejoice!
Light has come into the world!

The mountains sing;
the seas resound
to the praise of your name.
Salvation,
once promised, is found on
  earth!

The angels' song
rings in the air;
a child has been born.
Hallelujah!
The Saviour of the world is
  here!

First Sunday of Christmas

Sunday between 26 December and 1 January

ISAIAH 63:7–9; PSALM 148; HEBREWS 2:10–18; MATTHEW 2:13–23

Opening prayer

May the same Spirit
who brought those first
  worshippers
to a stable in Bethlehem
be the Spirit who draws us
  here,
as we bring our offering
of praise and service,
in this place, wherever we
  might be.

Adoration

We worship the birth of a baby,
and in doing so
acknowledge you, Lord,
reaching down to touch the
  earth
and bless it once again,
to walk within the garden
as previously in Eden.

We worship the birth of a
  Saviour,
an infant in whose fragility
lay all the signs of sacrifice:
born in humility,
growing in obedience
and into his kingdom
as scripture's Promised One.

We worship Jesus, Saviour
  and King.

Confession

So many searching
for fulfilment,
contentment,
answers to the question 'Why?'
So many blindly
walking this road,
not realising
the question's not 'Why?'
  but 'Who?'

Forgive us,
we who have answers
and the destination
for those who search,
but sometimes lack the faith
to share them.
Grant us courage
in our conversations
and, by your Spirit,
empower us,
that our words
might reflect the light
now revealed to the world
in our Saviour, Jesus Christ.

Thanksgiving

Thank you
for scripture fulfilled
in the birth of your Son.

Thank you
for prophets' voices
and your kingdom come.

Thank you
for eternal love
and redemption's song.

Thank you
for all broken lives
made whole again.

Second Sunday of Christmas

Sunday between 2 and 5 January

JEREMIAH 31:7–14; PSALM 147:12–20; EPHESIANS 1:3–14; JOHN 1:[1–9] 10–18

Opening prayer

This day is your gift,
freely offered,
accepted in gratitude,
proclaimed to the world.
This day is your gift;
thank you, Lord.

Adoration

Creator God, from whom love
flows into hearts,
who has chosen us
and cares for us,
we praise your holy name.

Jesus Christ, Son of God,
Word become flesh
dwelling among us,
sacrificed for us,
we praise your holy name.

Holy Spirit, breath of life,
power of God
living within us,
working through us,
we praise your holy name.

Confession

God of the journey,
you call us to follow you
without fear of stumbling,
your hand held out
to steady the weakest soul.
Grant us a faith strong enough
to take you at your word
and, should we struggle,
to know you're with us along
  the way.

God of the journey,
forgive our moments of doubt
and strengthen our hearts,
  we pray,
that we might have the courage
to share our faith with others,
speak up for what we know
  is right,
and keep our feet firmly
on the path we know
you would have us tread.

Thanksgiving

We are not grains of sand
upon the shore,
buffeted by sea and storm,
but individuals loved by you,
  our heavenly Father,
more intimately
than we could ever know.
Though from a distance
we seem small and frail,
your Spirit lives in
and through us;
guides us daily,
feeds and sustains us.

We are not grains of sand
but solid rocks used by you
for the building of your
  kingdom.
That you could use us
for such a glorious purpose
brings us to your feet
in praise and gratitude.

Year A

The Epiphany

6 January or first Sunday in January

ISAIAH 60:1–6; PSALM 72:[1–7] 10–14; EPHESIANS 3:1–12; MATTHEW 2:1–12

Opening prayer

The light of the world has
  come;
God's radiance covers the
  earth.
Hallelujah!
Darkness shall never prevail
while you, Lord, bring light
  into our hearts.
Hallelujah!

Adoration

Arise, shine, for the light of the
  world has come!

Darkness covers the face of the
  earth
but the radiance of your light
burns away its shadows,
illuminates the smallest corner
and heralds the start
of a new dawn
where hearts no longer fear,
souls might be set free
and sister shall walk with
  brother,
nation follow nation,
and kings and princes bow
  down in awe
before the one who comes
  to reign.

Arise, shine, for the light of the
  world has come!

Confession

We stand at your feet,
creation facing creator,
hearts laid bare by your light,
asking for mercy.
We come as a people in need
of assurance and grace.
We come as a people in need
of healing and peace.
We come dependent upon you.

Draw us close; fill us once
  more
with the flame of your Spirit,
that we might radiate your
  warmth
to a world grown cold,
speak your word with boldness
and draw others to your light.

Thanksgiving

For those who seek a Saviour,
we lead them, with gratitude,
to the stable,
to the one who was born
to bring freedom,
healing,
peace.

For those who seek assurance,
we lead them, with gratitude,
to the light,
to the one who opens eyes
to understanding,
wisdom,
truth.

For those who seek forgiveness,
we lead them, with gratitude,
to a love
beyond comprehension,
to wholeness,
mercy,
grace.

Year A

Baptism of Christ

Sunday between 7 and 13 January
ISAIAH 42:1–9; PSALM 29; ACTS 10:34–43; MATTHEW 3:13–17

Opening prayer
Spirit of God,
be with us
in the singing of our hymns,
the offering of our prayers
and the meeting of our lives.
Be the unity between us
and the power that ignites us
to be your light in this dark
  world.

Adoration
In the water of baptism
you were revealed
as God's own Son
and in the Spirit's power
you walked upon this earth.

And we ourselves,
washed in living water
and knowing forgiveness,
walk in your footsteps
through your Spirit's power.

God above us,
God with us,
God within us,
God flowing from us,
we praise your glorious name.

Confession

We whose hearts have known
  your love,
whose lives have been
  transformed,
whose hands have been used,
whose voices have been heard,
whose eyes have witnessed
the extent of your love,
have too often kept silent,
stepped back lest we be
  noticed,
ignored the opportunity to
  share
the truth that we believe.

Forgive our timidity;
grant us the courage
to testify to the power of your
  love,
so that others might be enabled
to become what they were
  meant to be.
We ask this through the one
  who loves us
more than we could ever
  know.

Thanksgiving

You who walked this earth
as servant,
  shepherd,
    friend to all;

You who talked of sin
and darkness,
  healing,
    forgiveness;

You who, crucified,
rose again
  for those
    here gathered;

You it is we praise and thank,
Son of God,
  Saviour,
    Lord and King.

Second Sunday of Epiphany

Sunday between 14 and 20 January

ISAIAH 49:1–7; PSALM 40:1–11; 1 CORINTHIANS 1:1–9; JOHN 1:29–42

Opening prayer

As we sing our hymns of
  praise,
listen to your word
and bring to you our prayers,
touch our hearts anew
that our spirits
might be revived
by your Spirit,
and our lives
more clearly point to you.

Adoration

There is no other name in the
  heavens
in whom we can find our
  salvation
except for Jesus Christ,
Son of God,
risen for us,
interceding for us,
here with us.
In you we find forgiveness;
in you we find wholeness;
in you we find the potential
to become the people
we were created to be.

There is no other name in the
  heavens
in whom we can find our
  salvation,
and to you alone, Jesus Christ,
  we bring our praise.

Confession

Lamb of God,
who takes away the sin of the
  world,
forgive us
for all we have done, and not
  done.

Lamb of God,
who takes away the sin of the
  world,
grant us peace
as your Spirit dwells in our
  hearts.

Lamb of God,
who takes away the sin of the
  world,
grant us love
to share with all who walk
  this road.

Lamb of God,
who takes away the sin of the
  world,
bring us joy
in our daily journeying with
  you.

Thanksgiving

When hearts are weary
and on our journey
we stumble and fall,
we cry to you for help
knowing that you hear,
and that your hearing will bring
healing,
  wholeness
    and peace.
You raise us up again
to firmer ground,
point the way ahead,
and equip us for the task.
Such love,
  patience
    and grace.
How can we not bring to you
our offering of thanks?

Third Sunday of Epiphany

Sunday between 21 and 27 January

ISAIAH 9:1–4; PSALM 27:1, 4–9; 1 CORINTHIANS 1:10–18; MATTHEW 4:12–23

Opening prayer

Lord God, our light
and our salvation,
illuminate this place
and all who meet here
with the brightness
of your presence.
Melt away all shadows
and bring into our hearts
the flame of true worship,
which nothing can put out.

Adoration

Jesus Christ,
light of this world,
you came into our darkness
as the dawning of a new day,
the warmth of your love
burning through morning mist,
scattering clouds,
revealing all that had once
been hidden from our eyes—
the beauty that surrounds us,
the earth that sustains us,
the heavens above us,
our place and purpose,
the one who made us.
As the dawning of a new day
you came into our darkness,
light of this world,
Jesus Christ.

Confession

You call us to follow
the path you have walked;
where there is hardship
to bring relief,
where there is sickness
to bring healing,
where there is sadness
to bring comfort,
where there is darkness
to bring light.

Forgive us when we are
reluctant disciples.
Grant us faith,
confidence
and passion
to be obedient to your call,
and feet that are willing to
  follow.

Thanksgiving

You, Lord, are our salvation,
the rock upon which we stand,
the light by which we walk,
the strength by which we
  overcome.
Therefore we shall live by faith
and fear no one!

Leader: To you alone, O Lord,
  we bring
**All: Our grateful thanks and
  praise.**

You, Lord, are with us always,
your loving arms encircling
and sheltering us from harm.
It is your song that we
  shall sing,
of forgiveness,
and God's kingdom
revealed upon the earth.

Leader: To you alone, O Lord,
  we bring
**All: Our grateful thanks and
  praise.**

Year A

Fourth Sunday of Epiphany

Sunday between 28 January and 3 February

MICAH 6:1–8; PSALM 15; 1 CORINTHIANS 1:18–31; MATTHEW 5:1–12

Opening prayer

In this place we are gathered,
with our joys and concerns,
in our wholeness and
  brokenness,
individuals and yet one body
drawn to you in worship.
In this place we are gathered
to share and learn together,
to build up one another
and bring to you this offering,
our sacrifice of praise.

Adoration

You are an amazing God
who would choose
the simple things of this world
to confound those
who call themselves wise;
who blesses the weak
and humbles the proud,
raises the lame,
restores sight to the blind.

You are an amazing God
who chooses the people
gathered here today
to be your witness
in this dark world,
to bring your peace
and sow seeds of love.

You are an amazing God
and we shall praise your name!

Confession

When we forget the blessings
  of each day,
whether living in poverty or
  plenty,
good health or poor,
sorrow or joy,
peace or conflict,
with family
or alone,
  forgive us.

Remind us that this day is a
  brief moment
in an eternity of your love
  and grace,
freed from all pain,
hearts filled with joy,
knowing your peace,
together
with you,
  for ever.

When we forget the blessings
  of each day,
good Lord, forgive us.

Thanksgiving

Where would we be without
  your light?
Losing our way in darkness.
Where would we be without
  your peace?
Caught up in this world's
  wisdom.
Where would we be without
  your love?
Looking for your warm
  embrace.
Where would we be without
  your word?
Searching this world for
  freedom.
Where would we be without
  your power?
Struggling in our weakness.
Where would we be without
  you, Lord?
Lost and in need of grace.

We give you thanks
for light, peace, love, word,
  power and grace.

Year A

Proper 1

Sunday between 4 and 10 February
(if earlier than the Second Sunday before Lent)

ISAIAH 58:1–9A [9B–12]; PSALM 112:1–9 [10]; 1 CORINTHIANS 2:1–12 [13–16];
MATTHEW 5:13–20

Opening prayer

This is your day
and we shall praise you
with all that is within us,
hearts, souls and voices
raised in worship
and adoration.
This is your day
and we shall praise you.

Adoration

Spirit of truth
who reveals to us the things of
    God,
we praise your name.

Spirit of wisdom
who inspires the words we
    have to speak,
we praise your name.

Spirit of power
who grants the courage we
    need to act,
we praise your name.

Spirit of love
who knows our nature and
    loves us still,
we praise your name.

Confession

The worship that pleases you
is not simply with our words
but with our lives and hearts.
The worship that pleases you
is to bring love and justice
where there is conflict,
healing and compassion
where there is need.

The worship that we offer
falls short of your ideal.
Forgive us when our lives
do not reflect our faith.
Give us a heart for all
to whom you would lead us,
and a willingness to serve,
that your name might be
  glorified
through the love that we show.

Thanksgiving

Son of God,
with thankful hearts
we follow you,
who walked this earth as
  prophesied
by scripture's timeless word
and opened up the kingdom's
  door
for all who walk inside;
who trod the road of sacrifice
and service for the world,
that all might know the
  kingdom's power
and none be left outside.
Son of God,
with thankful hearts
we follow you.

Year A

Proper 2

Sunday between 11 and 17 February
(if earlier than the Second Sunday before Lent)

DEUTERONOMY 30:15–20; PSALM 119:1–8; 1 CORINTHIANS 3:1–9; MATTHEW 5:21–37

Opening prayer

Father God,
here your children meet
with each other and with you.
Bless this time together,
our worship,
prayer and conversation.
Bless this new week,
its todays,
tomorrows
and opportunities.

Adoration

God of grace,
it is only through your love
that we can know that we are
  saved,
gentle Shepherd, who never
  lets us go.
Led by your Spirit,
we come into your fold
and shall remain with you
  for ever.

God of power,
it is by your strength alone
that we can follow your
  commands;
without your help we stumble
  on the road.
But you are gracious;
your hand is there to hold
and we shall walk with you
  for ever.

Confession

If we are here today
and know our hearts are not
  at ease,
for there is anger deep within,
  forgive us.
If we are here today
and know that words we
  have used
have caused another one to
  stumble,
forgive us.
Remind us of your love,
which joins hearts together
  in unity,
brings healing to relationships,
brings glory to your name.
Forgive us,
  renew us,
    refine us,
that our hearts
might overflow with you
and touch this world with
  grace.

Thanksgiving

We gaze at the world
in which we live
and see within
so much of your provision.
Seed scattered,
vulnerable upon the ground,
which germinates,
blossoms and bears fruit,
nurtured by the warmth
of the sun's shining rays
and gentle rain.
And your word,
sown in the rich soil of our
  hearts,
which germinates,
blossoms and bears fruit,
nurtured by the warmth
of your Spirit
and living water.
Thank you for love revealed,
and fruitfulness!

Year A

Proper 3

Sunday between 18 and 24 February
(if earlier than the Second Sunday before Lent)

LEVITICUS 19:1–2, 9–18; PSALM 119:33–40; 1 CORINTHIANS 3:10–11, 16–23;
MATTHEW 5:38–48

Opening prayer

In our meeting together,
be the peace between us,
the love surrounding us
and the joy that our hearts
  pour out.

In our leaving together,
may the love within us
and the peace between us
be the blessing that we give.

Adoration

The life we are called to live
is the life you have revealed
in your word—
to love as we are loved,
give as we receive
and bless as we are blessed.
The life we are called to live
is one of obedience
to the one
who has given everything,
that we might know
the true meaning of sacrifice,
the Son of God
to whom,
with Father and Spirit,
holy Trinity,
all praise is due.

Confession

You call us to reach out
to our neighbours,
some of whom
we would not willingly choose:
the difficult people,
troubled people,
angry people,
broken people,
hope-less people.
Then we remember
that these are the people
you spend your time and love
. upon.

Forgive our reluctance
to follow the path you trod
when it becomes
 uncomfortable.
Give us a faith that is true,
obedient to your word.
Through Jesus Christ alone,
who loves even us—
those cause him pain—
this we ask.

Thanksgiving

Thank you for those
who were good neighbours
 to us
when we were in need,
who gave of their time and self
to be your comforter
or brought a word in season
that lifted our weariness.

Thank you for those
who sowed the seeds of hope
into the garden of our hearts,
and by their encouragement
enabled faith to grow and
 flourish
and us to become the people
you always wanted us to be.

Thank you for good
 neighbours.

Second Sunday before Lent

ISAIAH 49:8–16A; PSALM 131; 1 CORINTHIANS 4:1–5; MATTHEW 6:24–34

Opening prayer

God of love, be with us now—
the love that dwells
  between us,
the love we share around us
and the love that we declare
to everyone who hears us.
God of love, be with us now.

Adoration

You have clothed this world in
  beauty,
from morning mist dissolving
  into summer day
to the splendid isolation of a
  mountain peak,
from flowers of the field in all
  their radiant hues
to butterfly emerging from
  chrysalis, all speak
of the artist's vision and
  creativity,
the loving brush strokes with
  which you paint.

And if you should take such
  care with these,
who are we to doubt the value
  that you place
on those whose hearts contain
  the maker's mark?
We shall not worry what
  tomorrow brings,
for even in sorrow you bring
  us joy
and we shall praise you for all
  good things!

Confession

Nothing is hidden from you,
  Lord;
your light shines
through the darkness of this
  world
into the shadows of our hearts.
You see our thoughts
and motives,
consider our words
and actions.
This must cause you sadness,
  Lord,
if it is our response
to all that you have done
  for us.
Forgive us, we pray,
and by your grace and mercy
bring us to that place
where your light might shine
  within
and reveal nothing but your
  eternal love
and our response of praise.

Thanksgiving

In you alone we put our hope,
God the Father, Creator,
  Sustainer,
who gives all good things,
seen and unseen.

In you alone we put our hope,
God the Son, Saviour,
  Redeemer,
who died for our sins
and rose again.

In you alone we put our hope,
God the Spirit, Teacher, Healer,
for by your power
the blind can see.

In you alone we put our hope,
Holy Trinity, three in one,
who moves us to sing
our thanks and praise:
'Hallelujah!'

Sunday Next before Lent

EXODUS 24:12–18; PSALM 2; 2 PETER 1:16–21; MATTHEW 17:1–9

Opening prayer

Into your presence we come,
your people gathering for
  worship
with this offering of praise
and the burdens on our hearts.
Bless our fellowship together,
and our going out into the
  world,
and may the blessing we
  receive
be the blessing that we share.

Adoration

On the mountaintop
your glory was revealed
to Moses and Israel
in swirling cloud
and consuming fire.
Law was written on hearts and
  stone,
a new relationship begun.

On the mountaintop
your glory was revealed
to Peter, James and John
in transfiguration
and blinding light.
Love was written on hearts of
  stone,
a new kingdom established.

On the mountaintop
your glory is revealed
and on valley floor
your mercy seen
in light and grace.
Living stones and loving hearts
are built on such a firm
  foundation.

Confession

For those times when our
words
do not reveal the faith we
profess,
forgive us, Lord.
For those times when our
actions
are not grounded in your love
and grace,
forgive us, Lord.

Soften our hearts;
bring back the fire
we remember from the start,
that wherever we journey
your name might be lifted up
in all we say and do.

Thanksgiving

Your word can be heard
above the sound
of this world's insistent voice.
Even your whisper,
sharper than a two-edged
sword,
can be discerned
as it cuts through the
confusion
of human wisdom,
bringing truth home to our
hearts.

Your word can be heard
as scripture
speaks directly to our lives,
when prophets' voices
challenge the way things are,
and when, through the silence
of meditative prayer,
your word takes root,
grows and blossoms in our
hearts.

We give you thanks that your
word can be heard!

First Sunday of Lent

GENESIS 2:15–17; 3:1–7; PSALM 32; ROMANS 5:12–19; MATTHEW 4:1–11

Opening prayer

God of glory and grace,
accept this offering of our
  praise
and the prayers that we shall
  bring.
Accept this offering of our lives
and the songs that we shall
  sing,
God of glory and grace.

Adoration

Your word reveals to us a
  simple truth,
that sin entered this world
through human folly
in believing we could be
  like you,
and permeated history
through envy, selfishness and
  greed.
Yet sin, which holds us tight
within its grasp,
cannot withstand a heart that
  is touched
by your grace through Jesus
  Christ,
cannot contend with living
  water
pouring into hearts and souls.

Your word reveals to us a
  simple truth,
that sin is defeated
and we can become
the people we were always
  meant to be,
by your grace through Jesus
  Christ.

Confession

Jesus, Son of God,
have mercy on us;
forgive the weakness of our
  faith.

Jesus, Prince of Peace,
have mercy on us;
forgive the anger we have
  caused.

Jesus, Good Shepherd,
have mercy on us;
forgive the selfish lives we
  lead.

Jesus, Life and Truth,
have mercy on us;
restore to us the love we knew.

Thanksgiving

This world tempts us
to believe the wisdom that
  comes
from human minds,
to have faith in no other thing.
But we have glimpsed the
  truth
revealed in scripture's words,
and we shall worship the Lord
  our God
and serve him alone!

This world tempts us
to believe we have control
of our destiny
and have no need of the
  divine.
But we have felt the touch
of Christ upon our hearts,
and we shall worship the Lord
  our God
and serve him alone!

Second Sunday of Lent

GENESIS 12:1–4A; PSALM 121; ROMANS 4:1–5, 13–17; JOHN 3:1–17

Opening prayer

This day is your gift to us,
a day of opportunities
to be used in your service.
Bless our coming together
and our departing,
that the love we discover
might radiate from our lives
and draw others to your feet.
This day is your gift to us;
may we make good use of it.

Adoration

Leader: Creator God
All: Let us sing your praise!

What more do we need to
    know about you, Lord?
From the moment we were
    formed
from the dust of this earth,
imprinted upon our mortal
    frames
was your precious hallmark,
that we might know
our true value in your eyes,
and know your love and grace.

Leader: Creator God
All: Let us sing your praise!

What more do we need to
    know about you, Lord?
There is nothing we can do
to make you love us more
or even make you love us less,
for you gave your only Son
to be born and give his life,
that we might know eternity
    with you.

Leader: Creator God
All: Let us sing your praise!

Confession

Dear Lord, you are our refuge,
keeping our feet steady,
watching over us, keeping us
from harm.

Leader: Where does our help
come from?
**All: From the Lord, maker of
heaven and earth!**

Dear Lord, you are our fortress
encircling us in safety,
granting peace when our lives
are not at ease.

Leader: Where does our help
come from?
**All: From the Lord, maker of
heaven and earth!**

Dear Lord, you are the Father
who knows us so well.
Forgive us when we stray from
your path;
in your mercy, bring us home.

Leader: Where does our help
come from?
**All: From the Lord, maker of
heaven and earth!**

Thanksgiving

For love beyond imagining,
stepping down from a
heavenly realm
to walk this fragile earth,
touch a vulnerable people
and shed such precious blood
for the sake of people like us,
accept this, our offering of
thanks.

For love that is so inspiring,
taking the role of a servant
in such humility,
washing feet, serving bread
and wine,
being available
for broken lives to be made
whole,
accept this, our offering of
thanks.

Third Sunday of Lent

EXODUS 17:1–7; PSALM 95; ROMANS 5:1–11; JOHN 4:5–42

Opening prayer

Come, let us sing to the Lord
  our Maker,
our rock and our salvation,
the great shepherd of his
  sheep.
We are the people of his
  pasture
and the flock under his care.
Come, let us sing to the Lord
  our Maker.

Adoration

Your love,
which breathed this world into
  being,
established a covenant people,
bringing them out of captivity
and into a promised land.
Hallelujah!

Your love,
which from the moment of our
  birth
has known and called us by
  name,
leads us out of this world's
  slavery
into the kingdom of God.
Hallelujah!

Your love,
poured into the heart of Jesus
who endured the nails of our
  sin,
defeated death to rise again
and causes our hearts to sing.
Hallelujah!

Confession

We are impatient, Lord,
a demanding people,
particularly when we pray,
thinking our time
more precious,
and our needs
much greater
than anyone else's.

Forgive us, Lord;
teach us patience,
unselfishness
and humility
to accept the truth
that you do answer prayer,
in your way
and in your time,
which is always
the right time.

Thanksgiving

Come, all who are thirsty,
says Jesus, our Lord;
come, all who are weak;
taste the living water
I freely give.
Dip your hands in the stream,
refresh body and soul,
drink from it,
wash in it,
depend on it,
for this water
will never run dry.

Come, all who are thirsty,
says Jesus,
and with thanksgiving
we draw close to the living
water,
and find our souls refreshed.

Fourth Sunday of Lent

1 SAMUEL 16:1–13; PSALM 23; EPHESIANS 5:8–14; JOHN 9:1–41

Opening prayer

May the good shepherd
who leads his sheep
gather us into his fold,
to feed on his word,
drink his living water
and in due course be led
to safe and green pasture.

Adoration

What have we to say of you,
  Jesus Christ,
we whose eyes have been
  opened
so that now we see,
we whose ears have been
  opened
so that now we hear?
You are teacher,
prophet,
healer,
friend of the friendless,
hope of the oppressed,
liberator.
You are these but so much
  more,
for you are the Love of God,
filling hearts and souls
  wherever you should pass.
You are the Word of God,
bringing truth and wisdom to a
  world that's lost.
You are the Son of God,
travelling the road that leads to
  a cruel cross.
You are this world's Saviour
and the reason we are
  gathered in this place.

Confession

Forgive those things we've
  done
that have caused you sadness,
and those things we ought to
  have done
that would have brought you
  joy.
In both we have failed
ourselves,
  and you.

Bring us back to that place
where our journey began,
when we said we would
  follow
wherever you would go.
Take us back to the cross
and lead us once again
from there
to where you would have
  us be,
so that we may become a
  blessing
to all we meet on this road.

Thanksgiving

Leader: For love beyond
  understanding
All: We thank you, Lord on high.

You chose a people for your own
to lavish love upon;
raised up prophets, priests and
  kings
to be the nation through which
Messiah would be revealed,
through whom your kingdom
  comes.

Leader: For love beyond
  understanding
All: We thank you, Lord on high.

You chose this people gathered
  here
to be your children,
loved and blessed, forgiven
through one who knew no sin,
the king of glory, crowned with
  thorns,
whose name we worship now.

Leader: For love beyond
  understanding
All: We thank you, Lord on high.

Fifth Sunday of Lent

EZEKIEL 37:1–14; PSALM 130; ROMANS 8:6–11; JOHN 11:1–45

Opening prayer

In our journeying toward the
  cross
we take a little time
for refreshment,
a drink of living water;
to feed on your word,
enjoying fellowship with you
and our travelling companions.
Bless this time together,
and when we leave this place
be our guide along the road,
  we pray.

Adoration

Sovereign Lord,
your hand has touched
the dry bones of our faith;
your word has breathed
new life where there was
  death;
your Spirit has raised
us up from where we lay;
your love has brought
us home and to your cross,
and by your grace
we stand forgiven, free.
Hallelujah!

Confession

Your forgiveness is total—
no notebook
or post-it note
to remind you of our sin.
You take our confession
offered with hands outstretched
and gently,
like the loving
heavenly Father that you are,
and put it to one side
to be forgotten.
No grudges, no itching for
  judgement,
no resentment or ill-will.
Not like us,
who find it easy to say 'sorry'
but so hard to forgive
absolutely.

Forgive us, Father,
that we are often more willing
to accept forgiveness
than to forgive,
more willing to accept your love
than to share it with those
who have hurt us.
Teach us to forgive
as you forgive.

Thanksgiving

For the faith of those
who have gone before,
we thank you.

For all who have
responded to your call,
we thank you.

For those who have given
their lives for you,
we thank you.

You are the resurrection
and the life,
and all who believe in you,
though they might know
sorrow or joy today,
will know life in all its
  fullness
in your eternity.

Year A

Palm Sunday

LITURGY OF THE PALMS: PSALM 118:1–2, 19–29; MATTHEW 21:1–11

LITURGY OF THE PASSION: ISAIAH 50:4–9A; PSALM 31:9–16; PHILIPPIANS 2:5–11; MATTHEW 26:14—27:66

Opening prayer

In this time of gathering
accept the offering that we
  bring,
the songs we sing,
hearts open in prayer,
ears attuned to your word,
your children journeying
to Easter and beyond.

Adoration

Jesus, Lamb of God,
when you walked this earth
you did not consider
heavenly equality,
though it was yours to choose,
but took the role of servant
and in humility
  and obedience
allowed the rough nails of
  our sin
to be hammered into your flesh
for the sake of our salvation.

And so it is
that we acknowledge you
as Lord of our lives
and Lord of all,
to the glory of God the Father,
Son and Spirit, three in one.

Confession

May we be listening always
for your familiar voice
and obedient to your call,
whether quiet whisper
in a sacred space
or thunder's roar
cutting through the bustle
of a city street.

Forgive us those times when
you ask us to stay alert
for your sake
and, eyes heavy,
like your disciples
we fall asleep.
Forgive us our
Gethsemane moments.
May we be listening always
for your familiar voice
and obedient to your call.

Thanksgiving

Some may mock
and others conspire against us
for the faith we profess
and the lives that we live,
but we shall praise and
   thank you,
our Lord and Saviour,
the rock upon which we stand,
the strength that we rely on,
our firm foundation
in a world that builds
on sand.

Year A

Good Friday

ISAIAH 52:12—53:12; PSALM 22; HEBREWS 10:16–25 [HEBREWS 4:14–16; 5:7–9];
JOHN 18:1—19:42

Opening prayer

This is a day of mixed
  emotions, Lord.
We are aware of the pain that
  Jesus endured
at the hands of soldiers
and upon the cross.
We think about the people who
welcomed Jesus into
  Jerusalem,
then shouted for his death.
We remember Peter's denial
and the disciples scattering in
  fear.
Yet we know that this
was a necessary process
for the work of salvation,
begun so long before,
to be accomplished.
Help us to understand
the path of love that Jesus
  travelled,
and the reason why it led to
  the cross.
Help us in our response,
as we learn what it means
to take up our cross
and follow.

Adoration

This is love:
that you spoke words of
  comfort,
walked with the unclean and
  unloved,
shared wisdom, bread and fish,
brought healing into lives
and challenged the status quo.

This is love:
that you spoke the word of
  God,
walked a painful road to the
  cross,
shared living water, bread of
  life,
brought salvation to this world
and died for the sake of us.

This is love:
it is a seed
sown in the ground,
which germinates,
blossoms
and spreads its sweet perfume
in the gentle breeze of your
  Spirit.

This is love.

Confession

You were a man of suffering,
acquainted with grief,
loved and despised
in equal measure.
You understand humanity,
know our failings
and love us still.

When we, like Peter
deny you by word or action,
  forgive us.
When we, like Judas, are
  tempted
to follow a different path,
  forgive us.
When we, like those in the
  crowd,
allow you to be crucified,
  forgive us.
Bring us to the foot of the cross
to stand next to the one who,
looking into your eyes,
  declared,
'Surely this was the Son of
  God!'

Thanksgiving

Gracious Father,
loving unconditionally,
whose heart
overflows with forgiveness,
accept this, our thankful
  prayer.

Gracious Son,
giving sacrificially,
whose body
bled for our salvation,
accept this, our thankful
  prayer.

Gracious Spirit,
flowing eternally,
whose breath
revives our faith and soul,
accept this, our thankful
  prayer.

Easter Day

ACTS 10:34–43; PSALM 118:1–2, 14–24; COLOSSIANS 3:1–4; JOHN 20:1–18

Opening prayer

Let us rejoice and be glad,
for our risen Saviour
has opened the gates of heaven
and invited us in!
Let us rejoice and be glad!

Adoration

Rejoice!
The stone is rolled away,
grave clothes neatly folded;
no more the smell of death.
Behold the empty tomb!

Leader: Hallelujah!
All: He is risen!

Rejoice!
Scripture has been fulfilled;
the sting of death is gone
and victory has been won.
Behold the risen Christ!

Leader: Hallelujah!
All: He is risen!

Rejoice!
The curtain's torn in two;
our God invites us in,
Christ's sacrifice enough
to wash away our sins!

Leader: Hallelujah!
All: He is risen!

Confession

Easter reminds us
that each time
we deny you,
another nail is sharpened,
and each time
we defy you,
into your hand it is hammered.

When faith is weak,
temptation strong
and courage fails,
forgive us, Lord.
Become again
that risen presence
within our hearts.

Thanksgiving

We give thanks to you, Lord,
for your living presence in our
   lives!

When we were walking in
   darkness
you were there;
when we were kneeling in
   weakness
you were there;
when we drew near feeling
   worthless
you were there;
when we were needing
   forgiveness
you were there;
when we were searching for
   mercy
you were there.

We give thanks to you, Lord,
for your living presence in our
   lives!

Second Sunday of Easter

ACTS 2:14A, 22–32; PSALM 16; 1 PETER 1:3–9; JOHN 20:19–31

Opening prayer

As we gather for worship
let us take a moment of calm
in the midst of this busy life
to reflect on the Easter
  message
of hope and new life.

(Silence)

Bless this time together, Lord,
our worship and our
  fellowship,
and bind us ever closer in your
  love.

Adoration

God of promise and God of
  hope,
through your great mercy
you have granted us new birth
through the death
and resurrection of Jesus
  Christ.
We praise your wonderful
  name!

God of glory and God of might,
through your great power
you have granted us new
  strength
to endure all things
through faith in our risen king.
We praise your wonderful
  name!

Confession

Forgive us, Lord;
we are not the Easter people
we should be,
living in the knowledge
of your mercy and grace.
Distracted by the world,
we fail to hear your voice;
we hide when faith is
  challenged
or wander from the path.

Grant forgiveness,
Lord, we pray.
Restore to us
the love that we first knew
and a faith that endures,
whether on this road
the sun should shine
or dark clouds gather.
May we be your Easter people.

Thanksgiving

We have not seen your face,
touched your side
or heard your voice first-hand,
as did your friends
gathered together
that first Easter time.
But we have seen your love
in those around,
felt the warming of our hearts
and known your grace
bring wholeness to broken
  lives.
So with Thomas
we cast all doubts aside
and, with everlasting gratitude,
acknowledge you as
our Lord and our God!

Third Sunday of Easter

ACTS 2:14A, 36–41; PSALM 116:1–4, 12–19; 1 PETER 1:17–23; LUKE 24:13–35

Opening prayer

Risen Lord,
be the presence we feel,
the love that we share
and the focus of our prayer,
in our gathering for worship
on this your day.

Adoration

It was always your will
that Israel should find
in Jesus Christ
the one who would bring them
    home,
lost sheep returning
to the shepherd who is their
    king.
And to that fold
would come others
from every nation upon earth,
as prophets had foretold,
including those gathered here
    today
in honour of your name.

Gracious God, we praise you
for the promise of scripture,
the depth of your love
and our Saviour, Jesus Christ.

Confession

Lord, we bring to you
the load we carry,
burdens that weaken,
all that makes us stumble.
But we shall not be
  overwhelmed,
for we come to you in prayer
knowing that you hear our cry
and, having heard, will answer.

Lord, we bring to you
the sin we carry,
our envy and pride,
all that drags us down.
But we shall not be
  overwhelmed
for we come to you in prayer
knowing that you hear our cry
and, having heard, will answer.

Thanksgiving

Whether we are strong
  or weak,
whether we are rich
  or poor,
whether we are wise
  or not,
whoever we are,
there is nothing we can do
to deserve that which was
accomplished
for us on the cross—
nothing we can do
except bow our heads in
worship.
For sins forgiven
and the Spirit given,
  we simply
and humbly thank you.

Fourth Sunday of Easter

ACTS 2:42–47; PSALM 23; 1 PETER 2:19–25; JOHN 10:1–10

Opening prayer

Gracious Father,
be the blessing
that warms us.

Precious Son,
be the passion
that moves us.

Holy Spirit,
be the power
that enables us.

Three in One,
be our unity,
that which joins us.

Adoration

Good Shepherd,
we lack nothing
when we follow your word
and your commands.
You know our names,
our needs,
the loads we bear.
By your grace
you find us where we are
and lead us to quiet waters
and greener pasture.
For your love,
compassion,
mercy and grace,
Good Shepherd,
we bring this offering of praise.

Confession

We are your body,
your church,
your witness in this world—
a fact we sometimes forget.
When your love is not seen,
compassion not shown,
grace not revealed,
a need unmet,
forgive us.

Enable our hearts
to reflect your love.
Enable our hands
to respond to need.
Enable our voices
to bring your peace,
that through our lives
others may be drawn
into your kingdom
and your name be lifted high.

Thanksgiving

Jesus, your love
is beyond our imagining,
enduring so much
for the likes of us—
  humiliation,
    rejection,
      pain,
even death on a cross—
so we might understand
that a crown of thorns
was a perfect choice
for a servant-king
dying for our sins
and rising again
to claim this kingdom
for his own.
Jesus, such love
is beyond our imagining:
receive our heartfelt thanks.

Fifth Sunday of Easter

ACTS 7:55–60; PSALM 31:1–5, 15–16; 1 PETER 2:2–10; JOHN 14:1–14

Opening prayer

Risen Lord, be the light
that shines upon us,
through us
and beyond us,
that the worship of our hearts
might be the worship of our
  lives,
this day and all days.

Adoration

You are the God
who calls us to be
a chosen people,
a living sacrifice,
a holy nation.

You are the God
who calls us to be
an Easter people,
light to the world,
travellers with you.

You are the God
who calls us to be
a servant people,
worshippers
in word and deed.

You are the God we serve!

Confession

To whom can we turn
when we stray from the path
and this world challenges
all that we hold dear?
To whom can we turn
when the walls we have built
start tumbling down
in the midst of a storm?

In you, O Lord,
and no other
will we take refuge,
our strong fortress
and deliverer,
our faithful God.
To you, O Lord,
and no other
will we bow our knee
and humbly ask for
forgiveness.

Thanksgiving

You are more
than teacher,
prophet,
miracle-worker,
leader of men.

You are
  the Way
that we shall follow,
  the Truth
that we shall follow,
  the Life
that we shall follow.

You are more
than we deserve,
and we give you thanks—
our Saviour,
Redeemer,
Healer,
Friend.

Sixth Sunday of Easter

ACTS 17:22–31; PSALM 66:8–20; 1 PETER 3:13–22; JOHN 14:15–21

Opening prayer

Creator God,
you are the life
that sustains us
and the hand that
claims us;
you are worthy of our praise.
Reveal yourself
in our gathering,
and by your Spirit
join hearts as one
in this, our joyful offering.

Adoration

Leader: Come, sing to the Lord.
All: How great is his name!

Your love surrounds us,
reaches and finds us,
fills us, spills over
in blessings around us.

Leader: Come, sing to the Lord.
All: How great is his name!

Your love forgives us,
restores and guides us,
takes us and daily
in service empowers us.

Leader: Come, sing to the Lord.
All: How great is his name!

Confession

Your commands
are not a burden
that we carry,
but the life
we freely live.

Forgive us when,
through deliberate
or careless talk
and action,
we cause you
and others pain.
By your Spirit
guide and direct us,
in thought,
word and deed,
that our lives
might better reflect
the faith that we proclaim
and become a blessing,
bringing glory to your name.

Thanksgiving

In our journeying with you
it is your hand
that stops us stumbling
or slipping on the path;
your word
that keeps us growing
and builds up our faith;
your power
that grants endurance
whatever happens next.
Thank you
for the adventure,
the destination
and the blessings received
in all our journeying with you.

Year A

Ascension Day

May also be used on the Seventh Sunday of Easter

ACTS 1:1–11; PSALM 47; EPHESIANS 1:15–23; LUKE 24:44–53

Opening prayer

This is your day
and we shall praise you!
This is your day
and we shall declare your
  name!
This is your day
and we shall worship
our risen, ascended Saviour,
Lord and King!

Adoration

You are Lord of the heavens,
Creator of all,
seen and unseen.
You reign over the nations,
seated on high
upon your throne.
You draw all people to you,
bring sight to the blind,
release closed minds.
You open your heart to us,
forgive our sin,
welcome us home.
You are Lord of the heavens,
Creator of all,
worthy of our praise.

Confession

Risen Saviour,
forgive those moments
when our faith is weak
and our journey plagued
by uncertainty and doubt.
Open our minds
as you did on the Emmaus
  road,
that scripture may confirm
the truth of who you are.
Open our eyes
in the sharing of bread and
  wine
to the invitation
of fellowship with you,
Risen Saviour, Lord and King.

Thanksgiving

For the hope
to which you call us,
imperfect though we are,
we thank you, risen Christ.
For your willingness
to accept us
simply as we are,
we thank you, risen Christ.

Take these lives,
transform us,
bless us
and revive us,
that we might better
serve you as our king.

For the hope to which you
  call us,
imperfect though we are,
we thank you, risen Christ.

Seventh Sunday of Easter

ACTS 1:6–14; PSALM 68:1–10, 32–35; 1 PETER 4:12–14; 5:6–11; JOHN 17:1–11

Opening prayer

God of mountain peak
and valley floor,
who knows our joys,
our sorrows,
our highs and lows,
who picks us up as we stumble
and sets us on the road again,
be the blessing we receive
and the blessing we give
as we join in fellowship
to praise your name.

Adoration

The one
whose hands created us
is the one
who lives within us,
the one
whose breath sustains us,
the one
who rose to life for us,
the one
whose arms embrace us,
the one
who longs that we might
be one
as he is one,
Father, Son and Spirit—
the three in one
whose praise we sing!

Confession

There are times, Lord
when doubts flood in,
and faith struggles
to keep our heads
above water.
Forgive our weakness
and grant us strength,
for you endured all this
and so much more—
scourged and hated,
humiliated and slaughtered,
yet rising victorious
to demonstrate the paradox
of strength through weakness,
love conquering all.
We are weak
but through the grace of Christ
we are strong,
and with your help
will daily overcome.

Thanksgiving

You are father
of the fatherless,
friend
to the outcast,
restorer
of the broken,
liberator
of the captive,
rescuer
of the fallen,
lover
of creation.

You are the one
whose name we praise,
whose truth we proclaim,
whose life we live;
you are our God
and we thank you.

Day of Pentecost

NUMBERS 11:24–30; ACTS 2:1–21; PSALM 104:24–34, 35B; 1 CORINTHIANS 12:3B–13;
JOHN 20:19–23

Opening prayer

Spirit of life, breathe on us;
Spirit of truth, speak to us;
Spirit of hope, inspire us;
Spirit of power, work
  through us,
today and all days.

Adoration

God of power and glory,
we praise your holy name.
Your Pentecostal fire
spread not from priest or king
but from ordinary lives
when through your disciples
you set this world aflame.
So fill this place, we pray,
that your Spirit's power
might be seen
through *these* ordinary lives.

Rekindle the fire in our hearts
that was lit when we first
  believed,
that we might become
a blessing to many.
God of power and glory,
we praise your holy name.

Confession

If our flame grows dim
and faith goes cold,
revive us, Lord, we pray.
Breathe upon the spark
that still remains;
stir again the embers
of our first love;
warm our hearts
and souls for worship.
Bring us once again
to where it all began,
that we might become
messengers of grace,
relighting your flame of love
throughout this dark world.

Thanksgiving

For the gifts of your Spirit
so freely given
to those who ask,
we offer up our thanks.

For wisdom
to discern your will
and knowledge
for the building of faith,
we offer up our thanks.

For healing
bringing wholeness to lives
and prophecy
to declare your living word,
we offer up our thanks.

For the gifts of your Spirit
so freely given
to those who ask,
we offer up our thanks.

Trinity Sunday

GENESIS 1:1—2:4A; PSALM 8; 2 CORINTHIANS 13:11–13; MATTHEW 28:16–20

Opening prayer

May the love of the Father,
the tenderness of the Son
and the presence of the
  Spirit
gladden our hearts
as we meet for worship,
and bring peace to our souls
today and all days.

Adoration

Creator God, we glimpse your
  beauty
in setting sun and mountaintop.
We sense your power in thunder
  crash,
lightning flash and ocean's roar.

Leader: Creator God
All: We praise you.

Precious Jesus, we see your love
stretched out upon a cruel cross.
We stand in awe at your sacrifice,
love poured out for humankind.

Leader: Precious Jesus
All: We praise you.

Holy Spirit, we see your power
in lives transformed and hearts
  on fire.
We listen for your still, small
  voice,
comforting, guiding, calling.

Leader: Holy Spirit
All: We praise you.

Confession

In our moments of doubt
and unbelief,
when worldly pressure
or circumstance
become the distance
between us,
draw near, we pray.

Remind us of the grace
that we first knew,
the Father's love,
the Spirit's breath.
Grant us courage,
a faith that endures
and the sure knowledge
that you are with us
today and always,
never further away
than a whispered prayer.

Thanksgiving

For the glory of the heavens
above us,
the majesty of the earth
surrounding us
and the mysteries of nature
amazing us,
we stand in awe and wonder
and offer you our thanks.

For your love which daily
blesses us,
the protection of your arms
embracing us
and the mystery of your grace
poured out for us,
we stand in awe and wonder
and offer you our thanks.

Proper 4

Sunday between 29 May and 4 June (if after Trinity Sunday)

GENESIS 6:9–22; 7:24; 8:14–19; PSALM 46; ROMANS 1:16–17; 3:22B–28 [29–31];
MATTHEW 7:21–29

Opening prayer

We listen
in the stillness of our hearts
and in this precious moment;
we listen
to the murmur of the world
beyond these walls;
we listen
prayerfully for the gentle
whisper of your call;
we listen
in the stillness of our hearts,
and in this precious moment
we listen...

Adoration

You are the solid rock
on which we stand,
the firm foundation
we build upon.
Rain may fall,
earth tremble,
storms blow,
but we are secure
in your strength,
our feet steady
on your path.
Your faithfulness
and enduring love
from generation
to generation
are the reason we are here
and the focus of our praise.

Confession

You have called us
as messengers
of grace and love,
to walk the road
you walked along,
to share your word,
sing your song.

We have failed you
if our message
is whispered,
our song
left unheard,
a melody unsung.

Forgive us.
Give us a voice
that can be heard
and the courage
to confess
with the song of our hearts
that you are our Saviour
  and King.

Thanksgiving

You lived and died
and rose again
not for one people,
but all people—
family,
  friends,
    disciples,
the curious,
  the envious,
    opponents,
every sinner
in every generation
needing forgiveness
and grace.

You lived and died
and rose again,
not for one people,
but this people,
your people—
who offer you grateful thanks.

Proper 5

Sunday between 5 and 11 June (if after Trinity Sunday)

GENESIS 12:1–9; PSALM 33:1–12; ROMANS 4:13–25; MATTHEW 9:9–13, 18–26

Opening prayer

God of the journey,
in our walk with you
may these times of rest
be an oasis in your company.
Grant peace and refreshment,
that in these moments
we might find sustenance
for the road ahead.

Adoration

You bless all who
in faith obey your call,
follow where you lead
and depend upon your grace.
If we count ourselves
among that number who,
like Abram, left his country,
people and father's house
to move to a foreign land,
you will bless our departing
and our arriving.

For your faithfulness
to every generation
who, in obedience,
travel this road with you,
we praise your glorious name.

Confession

May we never be afraid
to come to you in prayer,
bring those things
that trouble
or cause us pain
and lay them at your feet.

May we never be afraid
to come in faith,
kneel and reach out
to touch your hem
or grasp your hand,
knowing our needs are met.

May we never be afraid
to come to you as Lord,
acknowledge you
as Son of God
and in your strength
tell others of your grace.

Thanksgiving

To God alone we bring
the sweet melody
of our hearts,
a chorus of thanksgiving
to our creator,
  sustainer
    and saviour!
To the one
who breathes life
into this world we call home,
who calls out
to those counted as his own,
who blesses
whenever true love is shown.
To God alone we bring
the sweet melody
of our hearts,
a chorus of thanksgiving
to our creator.

Proper 6

Sunday between 12 and 18 June (if after Trinity Sunday)

GENESIS 18:1–15 [21:1–7]; PSALM 116:1–2, 12–19; ROMANS 5:1–8;
MATTHEW 9:35—10:8 [9–23]

Opening prayer

As we are gathered in your
  name,
be the peace that comforts,
the love that shines through,
the hope that sustains
and the blessing that pours
  out,
through the worship of our
  hearts
and the service of our lives.

Adoration

What can we offer you,
O Lord our God,
as we meet together
in this place?
What kind of sacrifice
is sufficient
for your forgiveness,
mercy and grace?

None but the offering
of our lives,
sharing a love that is
for ever making
broken people whole.

What can we offer you,
O Lord our God?
All that we are
and all that we shall ever be.

Confession

When our lives do not reflect
the words that we proclaim,
bring us back to that place
where we first found your
  grace.
There we received a Spirit
not of timidity
but of courage,
to tell out the news
that our Saviour is not dead
but lives,
that all might know
this essential truth—
that while we were still sinners
Christ died and rose again
for people just like us.

Thanksgiving

Thank you for the privilege
of being your messengers,
announcing the news
that your kingdom is here
just waiting to be found—
not in some faraway place
or heavenly space, but here
where we live and breathe
in the presence of Christ
  our King.
Here, where the sick are
  healed
and broken lives made whole.
Here, where your children
  serve
and love is shared with all.
Here, where you rule in power
and sin cannot control.
Here, where your people meet
responding to your call.

Thank you for the privilege
of being your messengers,
announcing the news
that your kingdom is here
just waiting to be found.

Year A

Proper 7

Sunday between 19 and 25 June (if after Trinity Sunday)

GENESIS 21:8–21; PSALM 86:1–10; ROMANS 6:1B–11; MATTHEW 10:24–39

Opening prayer

This day is your precious gift,
received with gratitude.
Direct our thoughts and
   actions,
that we might make best use
   of it
in the worship and service of
   our lives.
This day is your precious gift;
help us share it with joy.

Adoration

Your love is beyond the ability
of human words to express,
that you could love each one
   of us
enough to bear the cross.

Leader: Great is your name
All: And worthy to be praised!

Your peace is powerful enough
   to still
the storms that trouble our
   lives;
you lead us to calmer waters
where we can rest a while.

Leader: Great is your name
All: And worthy to be praised!

Your joy is the sweetness that
   brings a smile
to uplift a mournful heart,
and gives light enough to guide
   us through
when all around is dark.

Leader: Great is your name
All: And worthy to be praised!

Confession

When we forget
all you have done,
forgive us, Lord, we pray.

When we forget
the love you showed
and the wisdom of your words,
forgive us, Lord.

When we forget
the life you gave
and your Spirit in our hearts,
forgive us, Lord.

When we forget
your call to serve
and listen to this world,
forgive us, Lord.

When we forget
all you have done,
bring us to your feet
and grant mercy, Lord,
we pray.

Thanksgiving

Thank you for giving us a voice
that can be clearly understood
above the clamour of this
world;

a sharpened sword
cutting though the confused
cries
of those who would deny you;

authority
to speak the truth in your dear
name,
bringing light to this dark
corner;

a prophetic voice
and the courage to employ it,
that hearts might be touched
here and now.

Thank you for giving us a voice
that can be clearly understood
proclaiming your glorious
name.

Proper 8

Sunday between 26 June and 2 July

GENESIS 22:1–14; PSALM 13; ROMANS 6:12–23; MATTHEW 10:40–42

Opening prayer

May this be a precious space,
where all who are searching
might find the warmth
of your presence
and the love of your family
gathered here today.

Adoration

We sing your praises, Lord,
as we come to you in prayer,
trusting in your unfailing love.

We sing your praises, Lord,
as we walk with you each day,
sharing the blessings
that you give.

We sing your praises, Lord,
for such amazing grace,
poured out for all,
to set us free.

We sing your praises, Lord,
every moment we have breath,
our risen, ascended,
glorious Christ.

Confession

When temptation takes us
into a shadowy place
where normally
we would not go,
bring light
into our darkness,
dispel our fears
and bring us safely
home to you.
Forgive our tendency
for wandering
and straying from your path,
and place our feet firmly
where only you would tread.

Thanksgiving

In the uncertainties of this life
you are the one we can
  depend upon,
the one whose love will never
  leave us,
the one whose peace calms our
  restless souls,
the one whose hope is our
  confidence,
the one whose joy causes us to
  sing,
the one who is worthy of our
  praise.

In the uncertainties of this life
you are the one we can
  depend upon—
and we thank you,
Father, Son and Spirit,
glorious Trinity.

Year A

Proper 9

Sunday between 3 and 9 July

GENESIS 24:34–38, 42–49, 58–67; PSALM 45:10–17; SONG OF SOLOMON 2:8–13;
ROMANS 7:15–25A; MATTHEW 11:16–19, 25–30

Opening prayer

We are drawn to this place,
this sacred space,
to meet as family,
welcome strangers,
share in fellowship,
and offer lives in service.

We are drawn to this place,
this sacred space,
to worship you, our God.

Adoration

It was not
to the rich and famous,
the powerful,
intellectual
or influential
that you entrusted
your word,
but to fishermen,
outcasts and sinners,
ordinary people
  like us.

And to ordinary people
  like us
you have revealed
the things of heaven,
that we might also
become bearers
of good news.
So we praise you, Lord,
for revelation
and the eternal message
of your salvation.

Confession

We want to serve you—
show your love where
love demands to be shown;
be your touch where
lives might be made whole;
speak your word
to those who would deny your
  power;
be your light
and draw others to your
  throne.
Yet, we confess,
we hesitate to speak your
  name,
are daily tempted
to listen to this world's voice
and know our lives
do not reflect your holiness.

So once again
we come to you in humility
and in faith proclaim,
'Thanks be to God,
who forgives and restores us,
through Jesus Christ our Lord!'

Thanksgiving

When the journey
seems long,
strength fails
and we stumble
as we walk,
you raise us up,
  refresh,
    encourage,
      share our load.

Gracious Lord,
travelling companion,
precious guide
along life's way,
for your presence,
strength and help
we give you thanks today.

Proper 10

Sunday between 10 and 16 July

GENESIS 25:19–34; PSALM 119:105–112; ROMANS 8:1–11; MATTHEW 13:1–9, 18–23

Opening prayer

In your name and for your
  glory
we join together as one.
Accept the praise of our
  mouths,
the joy of our hearts
and the service of our lives
within this place
and throughout our daily lives.

Adoration

The seed of your word
scattered on fertile ground
germinates,
takes root,
puts forth branches
beneath which
no weeds can grow,
and then flourishes,
blossoms
and brings forth fruit.

For the beauty of your word
sown in hearts and souls
and a wonderful harvest to
  come,
for such divine nourishment
we praise you, Creator God.

Confession

Your word,
that lamp for our feet,
reveals to us
the stony ground
we often tread upon.
There, stumbling
in our weakness,
we reach out a hand
for you to hold,
asking simply
that you lead us
once again
to firmer ground,
toward that rock
upon which
our journeying began,
where we can rest
in safety.

Thanksgiving

Lord, we are truly blessed,
we whose hearts
have been set free
through Jesus Christ,
whose desire is to know him
    more,
feel his presence,
experience life in all its
    fullness.

Lord, we are truly blessed,
we whose lives
have been renewed
by your mercy and grace
and, by your Spirit,
enabled for service,
to be your hands
bringing healing
and your voice bringing
    comfort
wherever there is need.

Lord, we are truly blessed!

Proper 11

Sunday between 17 and 23 July

GENESIS 28:10–19A; PSALM 139:1–12, 23–24; ROMANS 8:12–25;
MATTHEW 13:24–30, 36–43

Opening prayer

It is good to meet together
for worship
and prayer.

It is good to take time together
for fellowship
in your name.

It is good to know your
  presence
and take that blessing
everywhere.

Adoration

From our rising
to our lying down,
you are with us
every moment of the day,
our reassurance
when storms assail,
our strength
when courage fails.

From our rising
to our lying down,
your light brightens
every step along the way,
our comfort
when darkness falls,
the peace
that calms our soul.

From our rising
to our lying down,
you are with us
always.

Confession

You have sown
fertile seed
into our hearts,
good Gardener,
and we, willingly
or by neglect,
allow weeds to grow
and spoil the beauty
of this small corner
of your garden.
Keep our hearts free
of that which hides
your love, we pray,
and prune away
all that hinders,
that others might see
only your beauty
blossoming
within.

Thanksgiving

Thank you, Lord, for your
  sustaining love,
with us as each day unfolds,
in our venturing out
and in our returning,
with the people we meet
and in our conversation,
in those moments of joy
and in our frustration.

Thank you for a love
that sustains us,
  revives us,
    and enables us
to be the people
you have called us to be—
servants of your word
and bearers of good news
in this, your beautiful world.

Proper 12

Sunday between 24 and 30 July

GENESIS 29:15–28; PSALM 105:1–11, 45B; ROMANS 8:26–39; MATTHEW 13:31–33, 44–52

Opening prayer

Heavenly Father,
be the love that dwells
  within us.

Precious Jesus,
be the peace that dwells
  within us.

Holy Spirit,
be the joy that dwells
  within us.

Glorious Trinity,
be the blessing that sustains us,
both here
and as we go into the world.

Adoration

To you we bring our praise,
gracious God,
for all you have done
throughout time,
of which we are
grateful inheritors.
For your love,
infinitely patient
with a rebellious people;
for prophets,
priests and kings
faithfully proclaiming your
  word;
for Jesus Christ,
our Saviour, your Son,
and the victory of the cross.
For all you have done,
gracious God,
to you we bring our praise.

Confession

When faith is weak
you strengthen us;
when we lose our way
you rescue us;
when we fall into sin
you forgive us.

Gracious God,
remind us,
lest we forget,
that your love is
unconditional,
moulding us
into what we could be,
blessing us
that we might glorify you.
For love beyond price
and grace that we treasure,
may our lives become
a thank-offering to you.

Thanksgiving

We are citizens
of a heavenly kingdom,
precious
beyond our ability to buy,
powerful
beyond human imagining,
enduring
beyond time to eternity.
Together
with the angelic host
we join voices
in a thanksgiving chorus
to make the heavens ring,
singing, 'Hallelujah!
For the Lord our God,
the Almighty, reigns!'

Proper 13

Sunday between 31 July and 6 August

GENESIS 32:22–31; PSALM 17:1–7, 15; ROMANS 9:1–5; MATTHEW 14:13–21

Opening prayer

Gracious Father,
bring your blessing
into this meeting of your
  people
gathered here today;
speak to our hearts
through the hymns we sing,
the prayers that are said
and the reading
and understanding of your
  word,
that we might go refreshed
into the world,
and through our lives
bring refreshment to others.

Adoration

You are the God of
  compassion,
bringing wholeness
into broken hearts and lives;
you are the God of provision,
bringing sustenance
to body and soul,
and with love we offer you
our sacrifice of praise.

You are the God of mercy,
granting forgiveness
despite our many failings;
you are the God of salvation,
bringing true release
from all that binds us,
and with love we offer you
our sacrifice of praise.

Confession

Forgive us,
for our lives are blessed
through the simple
act of prayer
and yet so often
we hesitate
  as if afraid to ask.
Grant us the faith
  and certainty to know
that what we seek
  in faith,
will be answered
through your great love
and in your good time.

Thank you,
for our lives are blessed
through the simple
act of prayer.

Thanksgiving

Thank you, Lord,
for showing us that love
has no boundaries or end
but listens,
has patience,
compassion, grace,
walks the extra mile
and gives without
counting cost.

Thank you for granting us
a heart for those you love
and a willingness
to step out in faith
and serve you,
by sharing your love with
  others.

Thank you, Lord,
for showing us that true love
can be ours,
both to know and to give.

Proper 14

Sunday between 7 and 13 August

GENESIS 37:1–4, 12–28; PSALM 105:1–6, 16–22, 45; ROMANS 10:5–15;
MATTHEW 14:22–33

Opening prayer

Father God,
you welcome us into your
  house,
and we in turn welcome you
  into our hearts,
praying that you might bless us
in our meeting for worship,
the enjoyment of fellowship
and our service in this place
and wherever you might
  take us.

Adoration

We will sing your praises
and proclaim your name
always
and to the ends of the earth.

We will tell of your mercy
and grace,
of burdens lifted,
chains released,
  forgiveness,
    new life,
      hope
        and peace.

We will sing your praises
and proclaim your name
for as long
as we have breath.

Confession

Forgive us, Lord,
when we discriminate
against rich or poor,
by colour and creed
or even attitude.
Forgive us, Lord,
when we do not share
the power of your
transforming love
or reach out and touch
where there is need.
Whenever our lives deny
the truth that we profess,
forgive us
and renew us, Lord, we pray.

Thanksgiving

In the warmth of a
    summer dawn
we are reminded
of your Spirit's presence
as we begin our journeying.

In the soft light of a
    summer morn
we are reminded
that your light illuminates
every step along our way.

In the beauty of a
    summer scene
we are reminded
that this world was painted
with love as well as colour.

In the ending of a
    summer day
we are reminded
of tomorrow's potential
as the setting sun goes down.

Thank you for your presence
    with us
from dawn to the end of
    the day.

Proper 15

Sunday between 14 and 20 August

GENESIS 45:1–15; PSALM 133; ROMANS 11:1–2A, 29–32; MATTHEW 15:[10–20] 21–28

Opening prayer

God of the dawning,
you are there when we
  awaken
and welcome in the day.

God of the morning,
you are present on our
  journey,
our helper on our way.

God of the noontime,
you are with us in our
  meeting;
in friendship we are blessed.

God of the evening,
you are in our relaxation,
our lying down to rest.

Adoration

Faithful God,
who chose one people
to receive your blessing,
that through them
you might be revealed
to all people,
we bless your wonderful
  name.

Faithful God,
who through one person,
Jesus Christ our Saviour,
brings mercy,
peace and salvation
to all people,
we bless your wonderful
  name.

Confession

You ask us
to be your presence
in this world,
to invite others
to your kingdom,
feed the hungry,
heal the sick,
and yet our words
do not reflect our faith.
This is our regret.

Forgive us
and cleanse our hearts,
that the words we speak
might be only those
that encourage,
bringing healing,
  wholeness,
    blessing
and glory to your name.

Thanksgiving

Thank you
for the ordinary people
who bring to our lives
wisdom, love,
a word in due season,
compassion,
peace.
Ordinary people
who through the Spirit's power
become extraordinary
in your service.
Ordinary people
who through the love of Christ
bring the presence of God
into our lives.
In giving
may they receive
and may their lives be truly
  blessed.

Year A

Proper 16

Sunday between 21 and 27 August
EXODUS 1:8—2:10; PSALM 124; ROMANS 12:1–8; MATTHEW 16:13–20

Opening prayer

We enter this place with
 thanksgiving
and come into your presence
 with praise,
giving thanks for your love
and faithfulness
toward every generation.
Shout for joy, all the earth!
Worship the Lord with
 gladness!
Know that he alone is God.
BASED ON PSALM 100

Adoration

You are our strength
when courage fails,
our protection
when waters rise,
our comfort
in storm and gales,
ever present
throughout our lives.

You are the truth
by which we walk,
the wisdom
that is our guide,
the message
of which we talk,
the bridegroom
awaiting the bride.

Confession

We would love to walk
the straight and narrow way,
but often end up wandering
on rough and stony ground.
Forgive our waywardness
and tendency to stray,
our lack of concentration
in our journeying with you.
Renew our sense of purpose
in this and all our days,
and keep our eyes more
  focused
on the one who is our guide.

Thanksgiving

Father God,
you reveal yourself
in many ways,
so that many
might know you as Lord.
You are found
written within scripture's
  words,
in the whisper of your voice
and the wonders of this world.
You are found
in the greeting of a friend,
a selfless act of love
and a simple word of prayer.

Father God,
you reveal yourself
in many ways;
receive our thanks and praise.

Proper 17

Sunday between 28 August and 3 September

EXODUS 3:1–15; PSALM 105:1–6, 23–26, 45C; ROMANS 12:9–21; MATTHEW 16:21–28

Opening prayer

Bless this meeting of our lives,
the offering we bring
of body, mind and soul.
Bless the service that we give
within this fellowship
and wherever we might go.
Bless this meeting of our lives.

Adoration

Leader: You are a mighty God!
All: And worthy of our praise!

We will proclaim your name,
tell of your wonders,
share your mystery,
truth and wisdom,
seek your presence always.

Leader: You are a mighty God!
All: And worthy of our praise!

We will glory in your name,
walk in your footsteps,
listen to your word,
trust and obey,
sing your praises always.

Leader: You are a mighty God!
All: And worthy of our praise!

We will serve in your name,
show your compassion,
give generously,
carry our cross,
show your mercy always.

Leader: You are a mighty God!
All: And worthy of our praise!

Confession

If our lives do not always
bring you joy,
Lord, forgive.
You brought peace, patience,
forgiveness and grace
to a world not at ease
  with itself.
We bring impatience,
intolerance and fear,
none of which bring glory
  to you.

If our lives do not always
bring you joy,
Lord, forgive,
and restore to us
the love we first knew,
that followed
wherever you led,
and obeyed
whenever you called.
Lord, forgive.

Thanksgiving

Lord, you came
to call not just a few
to be your disciples
and walk with you
in Galilee,
but to be known
among all nations
as Lord and King.

Lord, you came
to become the Saviour
not just of the people
among whom you
were born and lived,
but of all who
take up their cross
and follow you.

Thank you, Lord—
you came for us.

Year A

Proper 18

Sunday between 4 and 10 September

EXODUS 12:1–14; PSALM 149; ROMANS 13:8–14; MATTHEW 18:15–20

Opening prayer

In this sacred space
we bring to you
our hymns and songs,
prayers and petitions,
our fellowship
and offerings,
to you, our Lord and King.

Adoration

We bring to you
a new song
written on our hearts,
a song of praise
and thankfulness
for all that you have done
in those lives you call your
   own,
whose hearts have been
   transformed,
who kneel before your throne.

We bring to you
a new song,
a joyful melody
echoing a heavenly chorus.
'Hallelujah! Salvation,
glory and power
belong to our God!'

Confession

Refresh our lives, Lord,
in your living water,
and we shall know that we
  are clean.
For actions we regret,
words spoken in haste,
relationships hurt,
trust abused,
  jealousy,
    envy,
      greed,
forgive us,
and restore that
which we have broken,
that your name might be
  glorified
through our words
and through our actions.

Refresh our lives, Lord,
in your living water,
and we shall know that we
  are clean.

Thanksgiving

For the joy of fellowship,
family together,
sharing thoughts,
concerns
and joys,
we thank you.

For your presence here with us,
encircling our lives,
your Spirit
in hearts
and souls,
we thank you.

For our daily walk with you,
the whisper of your voice
bringing hope,
wisdom
and grace,
we thank you.

Proper 19

Sunday between 11 and 17 September

EXODUS 14:19–31; PSALM 114; ROMANS 14:1–12; MATTHEW 18:21–35

Opening prayer

Bless this time of worship,
O Lord, we pray.
Be the peace we seek
in busy days,
the strength to go on
when spirit fails,
the wisdom we need
to live our lives,
the love that we share
in this, your house.
Bless this time of worship,
O Lord, we pray.

Adoration

Leader: Lord, our Lord
**All: How majestic is your name
in all the earth.**

God of mountain splendour,
glorious skies and mountain
  stream,
God of nature, new birth,
wakening spring and
  summertime,
we bless your wonderful
  name.

Leader: Lord, our Lord
**All: How majestic is your name
in all the earth.**

God of awesome power,
whose word the elements
  obey;
God of redeeming love,
who brings us to a promised
  land,
we bless your wonderful
  name.

Leader: Lord, our Lord
**All: How majestic is your name
in all the earth.**

Confession

Help us to love as you love,
to accept each person
for who they are,
precious in your eyes.
Forgive the prejudice,
intentional or not,
that causes us
to turn aside,
ignore the need
or walk away.
Help us to love as you love,
to accept each person
for who they are,
just as you have loved us.

Thanksgiving

You are the source
of our forgiveness
when the lives we lead
do not reflect
the words that we profess.

You are the strength
we are searching for
when faith is weak,
as you draw us to
your loving arms to bless.

You are the hope
that we inherit
of a kingdom
in heaven and on earth,
one that will never cease.

You are the source
of all that we are
or ever could be,
and to you we bring
this offering of our thanks.

Year A

Proper 20

Sunday between 18 September and 24 September
EXODUS 16:2–15; PSALM 105:1–6, 37–45; PHILIPPIANS 1:21–30; MATTHEW 20:1–16

Opening prayer

Bless this time of fellowship,
the opening of our hearts,
the hymns that we shall sing,
the prayers that will be shared.
Bless this meeting of our lives
and fill them with your peace,
and as we leave this place
be the blessing that we give.

Adoration

Leader: Lord of each moment
All: Be with us through this day.

You are Lord of each moment
from our rising to our lying
   down,
every step along our way,
our travelling companion
walking beside us on a familiar
   road.

Leader: Lord of each moment
All: Be with us through this day.

You are Lord of each moment.
In our thinking and
   conversation
your Holy Spirit inspires
and your gentle whisper
   guides,
accepting our burdens and
   sharing our load.

Leader: Lord of each moment
All: Be with us through this day.

Confession

Lord, forgive us
if we should ever
put you to the test,
when life is hard,
we're far from home
or the burden is too heavy
to carry alone.
Draw us close;
renew our faith in the one
who brings people
from wilderness
and troubled waters
into a promised place.
In our walk of faith
may we make
that journey too,
finding the peace
and contentment
that only come from you.

Thanksgiving

For all who stand firm
when faith is tested
and are not afraid
to confess your name
even when persecuted,
we give you thanks.
We ask for strength
should we be asked
to walk that thorny path.

For faithful saints of every age
who with Paul declare,
'To live is Christ
and to die is gain',
we give you thanks.
Bless their sacrifice
and bless all whose faith
has been brought to birth
by being in their presence.

Proper 21

Sunday between 25 September and 1 October

EXODUS 17:1–7; PSALM 78:1–4, 12–16; PHILIPPIANS 2:1–13; MATTHEW 21:23–32

Opening prayer

Father, Son and Spirit,
Holy Trinity,
present wherever hearts
are open and souls laid bare,
bless those gathered here today
for worship, fellowship and
  prayer.
Bind our hearts as one
as you are one—
Father, Son and Spirit,
Holy Trinity.

Adoration

Father God,
be the oneness that exists
  between us,
the focus of our lives and
  worship,
our unity of faith.

Precious Jesus,
be the peace that is shared
  between us,
the compassion we show to
  others,
our unity of love.

Holy Spirit,
kindle the flame that burns
  within us,
the light that will shine in the
  darkness,
our unity of hope.

Confession

You call us to unity,
to be of one mind
with our brothers
and sisters in Christ,
yet sometimes we struggle
with relationships,
a little reminiscent of
the world
in which we live.

Forgive us, Lord,
for within the Godhead
we see a oneness
that we should imitate.
Grant us the grace to love
those whom we find
  challenging
and the wisdom to know
when it is our turn to say
  sorry.

Thanksgiving

Your love does not fade
even as we choose
a different path
and are persuaded
to put faith aside
and pick up instead
forbidden fruit.

Your love is constant
and accepting.
Your love is merciful
and forgiving.
Your love is grace-full
and inspiring.
Your love is all we are not
and everything you are,
and we thank you,
our loving God and king.

Gracious God,
we offer grateful thanks
for all whose lives
have been touched by
  your love.

Proper 22

Sunday between 2 and 8 October

EXODUS 20:1–4, 7–9, 12–20; PSALM 19; PHILIPPIANS 3:4B–14; MATTHEW 21:33–46

Opening prayer

In this time of worship
bring your peace
to busy lives,
to those who worry,
who are afraid
or ill at ease.
May we all find rest
in your presence,
hear your gentle whisper
and feel your touch
upon our lives.

Adoration

The heavens declare your
  glory,
the skies exalt your name;
and though no anthem's sung,
no sermon written
or candles lit,
within the beauty of dawn
  chorus,
sun rising,
  stars at night,
lies more theology
than in any hymn that we
  could sing.
So we behold your glory
and in our hearts
join with the heavens
in rejoicing.

Confession

In our journeying with you,
 Lord,
keep us safely on the road,
avoiding the distractions that
seem to populate our day,
and in those times we stumble
may yours be the hand we
 hold,
as, seeking your forgiveness,
we step back into the world.

Thanksgiving

This world would have us
 believe
that true happiness comes from
 possessions
and that those who find
 contentment
with the simple things of life
 are wrong.
Yet to such as these you came,
and such as these you sent,
to herald a kingdom
in which to lose all things
is to gain everything,
and where true happiness
comes from the possession
of nothing
 but this—
to know Christ Jesus
and the power of his
resurrection
in our hearts and lives.

Accept now these thankful
 hearts,
and use them in the building
of your kingdom in this place.

Year A

Proper 23

Sunday between 9 and 15 October

EXODUS 32:1–14; PSALM 106:1–6, 19–23; PHILIPPIANS 4:1–9; MATTHEW 22:1–14

Opening prayer

God of this and every new day,
of sunrise and sunset,
be the focus of our worship,
at the centre of our fellowship,
a guide for our footsteps
and the peace to calm us
every hour of this day,
and as we lay our heads to
   rest.

Adoration

This day
and all days
we shall praise your name
and tell of all you have done.
For if we do not share your
   truth
through our lives and words,
how will they know?

This day
and all days
we shall seek to live
a life that reflects the love
and mercy that you have
   shown us
and to become your lights
within the world.
This day
and all days.

Confession

You have called us
to be your people,
to follow where you lead,
be obedient to your word
and bring your good news
wherever we might go.

Forgive the impatience
and lack of faith
that cause us to stumble,
preferring our way to yours,
relying on human wisdom
rather than the truth
that comes from you.

Draw us back into your arms,
as prodigals to our Father,
and grant us patience,
perseverance
and a childlike faith
in our journeying with you.

Thanksgiving

Thank you for those
who, by their example,
have been a light
on our journey with you;
those whose guidance
has inspired us,
whose enthusiasm
has infected us,
who live each day
in the knowledge that it
  matters.

Bless such faithfulness
wherever it is shown,
where lives become
an offering,
your word becomes
transforming,
and light is brought
into this dark world.

Proper 24

Sunday between 16 and 22 October

EXODUS 33:12–23; PSALM 99; 1 THESSALONIANS 1:1–10; MATTHEW 22:15–22

Opening prayer

We draw near to you in
  worship
with this offering of praise,
our prayers for those in need
and our lives dedicated to your
  service.
Bless this time of fellowship,
and may the blessing we
  receive
be the gift that we share
as we leave this place.

Adoration

Leader: You are Lord
All: And we will praise you.

You are Lord
of this life
and eternity;
nothing can be
hidden from your eyes.

Leader: You are Lord
All: And we will praise you.

You are Lord
and Creator
of all that we see,
and yet you walked
the paths we tread.

Leader: You are Lord
All: And we will praise you.

You are Lord
and Saviour
who died for the sake
of all who are
gathered here today.

Leader: You are Lord
All: And we will praise you.

Confession

Teach us your way, Lord,
that we might follow
more closely
and know more surely
that you walk with us
not only on
the mountaintop
but also on the valley floor.

Teach us your way, Lord;
forgive our hesitance
and fear of the terrain.
Guide us, hold us;
let our footsteps
be steady,
our fear dispelled,
and may each day
be an adventure
in faith with you.

Thanksgiving

Thank you, Lord,
that we are chosen
to share the good news
and point the way to you.

Thank you, Lord,
that in our labours
we can show your love
in everything we do.

Thank you, Lord,
that through your power
we can do all things;
your Spirit sets us free.

Thank you, Lord,
that we are chosen
to live by your word
and reveal your glory.

Proper 25

Sunday between 23 and 29 October

DEUTERONOMY 34:1–12; PSALM 90:1–6, 13–17; 1 THESSALONIANS 2:1–8;
MATTHEW 22:34–46

Opening prayer

Lord God, you are worthy of
  our praise,
for your grace offered to us
when we were far away,
and love bestowed on us
at the dawning of each day.
Lord God, you are worthy of
  our praise.

Adoration

We shall praise you, Lord,
with all of our heart,
this and every day.

You are the one
who loves us,
rescues
and restores us.

You are the one
who heals us,
blesses
and forgives us.

You are the one
who leads us,
teaches
and empowers us.

We shall praise you, Lord,
with all of our heart,
this and every day.

Confession

When our faith is weak
and we are tempted
to seek an easier way,
forgive us, gracious Lord.
You did not turn away
from confrontation
but, for our sake,
walked to the cross
and beyond,
that we might know
the power of love
and live it day by day.

May we know your strength,
so that in our weakness
we might be prepared
to stand up for the faith
that we profess,
and that your name
might be lifted high.

Thanksgiving

For your faithfulness
to generations who have
  followed you,
we thank you.

For your patience
with those of us who fail you,
we thank you.

For your grace,
freely given to all who come
  to you,
we thank you.

For your love,
which compels us to worship
  you,
we thank you.

Fourth Sunday before Advent

Sunday between 30 October and 5 November

JOSHUA 3:7–17; PSALM 107:1–7, 33–37; 1 THESSALONIANS 2:9–13; MATTHEW 23:1–12

Opening prayer

Ever-loving God,
we meet for worship
and fellowship
as your children,
to proclaim your glory
in this sacred place,
and walk with you
wherever we are led.

Adoration

To you, O Lord, we bring
our offering of praise,
to the one who hears
a people's cry,
brings release
from captivity,
deliverance
from desert places,
and from parched earth
brings forth living water,
abundant harvest
and new birth.
To you, O Lord, we bring
our offering of praise.

Confession

Forgive us, Lord,
when pride
is more visible than
humility;
appearance
more important than
substance;
and faith
takes second place to
opinion.

Remind us often
that Jesus
lived to bring glory
to you,
endured
suffering and death
for us,
and rose again
so that we might know
life
in all its fullness.

Thanksgiving

Thank you for the invisible
  people,
who live their Christian lives
in quiet and unassuming ways,
who have a heart for others,
who practise hospitality,
care for the needy,
befriend the lonely,
offer encouragement,
are dependable,
and have time to listen
and time to pray.

Thank you for the invisible
  people,
often unacknowledged,
without whom your kingdom
would be incomplete.

All Saints Day

1 November or the first Sunday in November

REVELATION 7:9–17; PSALM 34:1–10; 1 JOHN 3:1–3; MATTHEW 5:1–12

Opening prayer

We join with your saints
of every generation
in our offering of worship
and the service of our lives,
in this place and wherever
you might lead.

Adoration

For the blessings of the saints
who have preached your word
from generation to generation,
and then within our hearts
found such fertile ground.

Leader: For these, your saints
All: Bless their faithfulness.

For the blessings of your saints
who have shown your love
from generation to generation,
until it touched our hearts,
warmed and softened them.

Leader: For these, your saints
All: Bless their faithfulness.

For the blessings of your saints
who have shared your grace
from generation to generation,
until it filled our hearts,
changed and transformed
   them.

Leader: For these, your saints
All: Bless their faithfulness.

Confession

How soon we forget
the names of those
who taught your word
when we were young,
in often simple ways
but sowing seeds of faith.

Forgive us, Lord,
and bless all those
who give of their time
in sowing seeds
that may one day
take root,
blossom and flourish,
to be harvested by you.

Thanksgiving

Your saints are not always
  visible;
they work in the background,
encouraging;
they work in the night-time,
praying;
they work on the front line,
directing;
they work with the suffering,
healing;
they work in the war zone,
peacemaking;
they work in the day-time,
helping.

Your saints are not always
  visible,
but they are still your saints,
for which we thank you, Lord.

Third Sunday before Advent

Sunday between 6 and 12 November

JOSHUA 24:1–3A, 14–25; PSALM 78:1–7; 1 THESSALONIANS 4:13–18; MATTHEW 25:1–13

Opening prayer

Into your presence we come,
bringing the worship of our
  hearts;
your children in fellowship
with their heavenly Father,
bringing this offering of praise
and the service of our lives.

Adoration

In every generation
your name has been lifted
  high,
your faithfulness proclaimed
through prophet, priest and
  king.
And to the chorus
of your saints from every age
we add the harmony of our
  praise.
For you have brought us
from wilderness places
into green pastures
and a safe place
within your kingdom,
where your love,
grace and peace
belong to all who serve you
as Lord and God.

Confession

We are often poor servants
in your kingdom, Lord;
forgive our reluctance
to share your load.

May our hearts always be
  ready
to be troubled by injustice.
May our hands always be
  ready
to share the burden of a
  stranger.
May our feet always be ready
if asked to go the extra mile.
May our pride always be ready
to be humbled before we fall.
May our love always be ready
to be shared with those in
  need.
May our lives always be ready
to be a lamp in this dark world.

We are often poor servants
in your kingdom, Lord;
forgive our reluctance,
and inspire us, we pray.

Thanksgiving

We give you thanks
for every generation
that has passed on
the good news
that you,
Creator of the universe,
did not rest
once that work
was completed.
but continue
unceasingly
within human hearts,
creating the people
we were meant to be,
through mercy, grace
and our Saviour, Jesus Christ.

Second Sunday before Advent

Sunday between 13 and 19 November

JUDGES 4:1–7; PSALM 123; 1 THESSALONIANS 5:1–11; MATTHEW 25:14–30

Opening prayer

It is good to be in your
  presence, Lord,
in this oasis of peace
within our busy week.
Speak to us
through worship and prayer,
and in moments of reflection.
Speak to us
as we read your word
and share fellowship together.
It is good to be in your
  presence, Lord.

Adoration

We rejoice in the sure
  knowledge
that there is a purpose
to the lives we lead,
and the history
that we in part still write
is contained within your plan
for the redemption of this
  earth.
Your desire is for all people
to acknowledge you as Lord
and to know that love came
  down
to walk among a sleeping
  people
who saw and failed to
  recognise,
as does a slumbering world
  today,
the divine within the Son.

We rejoice in the sure
  knowledge
that you will come again,
and pray that we may be found
not sleeping but awake
to welcome home our risen
  Lord.

Confession

Forgive our busyness, Lord;
slow down our steps,
steady our breath
and calm our thoughts.
May we take longer
to reach our
destination,
and in the
journeying
may we discover
the quiet whispers
of another country
that we have walked
but never seen before,
where you can be found.
Forgive our busyness, Lord;
slow down our steps.

Thanksgiving

As this day unfolds,
may it be centred
not on our desires
but on our willingness
to become
  your voice,
your hands
  and feet,
your love,
  compassion
and peace.
As this day unfolds,
may it become
a 'thanks-living'
offering to you.

Christ the King

Sunday between 20 and 26 November

EZEKIEL 34:11–16, 20–24; PSALM 100; EPHESIANS 1:15–23; MATTHEW 25:31–46

Opening prayer

We will enter your gates
with thanksgiving,
lifting high your name
not only in this place
but in our daily lives,
that this world might know
our God is worthy of all praise.

Adoration

Oh, that the world
might acknowledge
your name
and join with us
in worship
and praise.

Oh, that the world
might recognise
its need
and look to you
for forgiveness
and grace.

Oh, that the world
might comprehend
your love
and turn to you
for salvation
and peace.

Confession

For all those times
we simply turned aside
and looked the other way
when faced by need,
forgive us.

For all those times
we could have said something
and brought a little comfort
but stayed silent,
forgive us.

For all those times
a neighbour was lonely
and, rather than visit,
we shut our door,
forgive us.

Unlock our hearts;
let love pour out
and overflow,
through your grace
and mercy, we pray.

Thanksgiving

Shepherd-king,
you lead us
to green pastures
and safekeeping
in your kingdom,
welcoming all
who follow
and acknowledge
you as Lord.

For such love
and faithfulness,
generation
  to
generation,
and your care for
all who are
the sheep of your flock,
we thank you.

Year B

Year B

First Sunday of Advent

Sunday between 27 November and 3 December

ISAIAH 64:1–9; PSALM 80:1–7, 17–19; 1 CORINTHIANS 1:3–9; MARK 13:24–37

Opening prayer

Here we are again, Lord,
your children at your feet.
May this be a blessed time,
a precious time,
a getting-to-know-you-better
  time,
a family time.
Here we are again, Lord;
bless us as we meet.

Adoration

A light shines
through the darkness,
and hope comes
to those who
wait patiently
for their salvation
to be revealed.
For your promises
will be fulfilled
both in this world
and in the next.
Human wisdom
withers away,
but your word,
once received,
endures eternally.

Confession

There is a fire
within our hearts
ignited by
your love and grace,
which we
carry with us
on our walk with you.

Forgive us
when that flame
is dampened
by the temptations
of the day.
By your Spirit's breath
revive us,
Lord of light and life,
we pray.

Thanksgiving

In this season
of Advent and expectation,
may the lives we live
and the words we speak
be focused on
thanksgiving,
even if this world,
as in days gone by,
would rather choose
to ignore your coming.
Let our witness
and testimony
be a compass,
pointing toward
a different
and altogether
more glorious
destination.

Second Sunday of Advent

Sunday between 4 and 10 December

ISAIAH 40:1–11; PSALM 85:1–2, 8–13; 2 PETER 3:8–15A; MARK 1:1–8

Opening prayer

As people walk by
to purchase for those they love
gifts that, in days to come,
will fade from memory,
within this place we gather
in celebration of your loving
 gift
to all of humankind,
remembered this and every
 day
by all who have welcomed
Christ Jesus into their hearts.

Adoration

In the lonely places,
the wilderness
where we stand forlorn,
windswept and alone:

Leader: A voice calls out,
All: Prepare a way for the Lord.

In the dark places,
the shadows
where we hide our fears
and embrace our tears:

Leader: A voice calls out,
All: Prepare a way for the Lord.

In the comfortable places,
the valleys
we have walked before,
where we feel secure:

Leader: A voice calls out,
All: Prepare a way for the Lord.

Confession

We have a promise,
a God-given promise
that will not fail—
of a new heaven
and a new earth,
where love
and righteousness
reside.
May our lives reflect
that promise
and be found
spotless
on that glorious day.

God of love
and mercy,
pour your living water
into these hearts;
cleanse and refresh them
that they might
overflow in praise.

Thanksgiving

In the streets we walk
and the places we go,
with people we meet
and decisions we make,
thank you for being our guide,
O Lord.
Take us to places
where you would go;
give us words
that you would say;
so that in this Advent season
of promise and preparation,
we might gratefully point
  the way
to the one who takes away
the sin of the world.

Third Sunday of Advent

Sunday between 11 and 17 December

ISAIAH 61:1–4, 8–11; PSALM 126; LUKE 1:46–55; 1 THESSALONIANS 5:16–24;
JOHN 1:6–8, 19–28

Opening prayer

At the rising of the dawn
and the setting of the sun
we will rejoice in the Lord.

In the busyness of the day
and the quieter times within,
we will rejoice in the Lord.

In the joining of our lives
and the fellowship we enjoy,
we will rejoice in the Lord.

Adoration

You came to this world
for the poor in spirit,
the broken-hearted,
those held captive,
those lost in sin.

You came to this world
to bring good news
and wholeness into lives,
to bring release
and to forgive.

You came to this world
to guide your people
from a desert place
to a kingdom
of love and grace.

You came to this world
to show how far love
is prepared to go,
and, on a cross,
showed heaven on earth.

Confession

When we trust the wisdom of
  this world,
straying from the pathway
you would have us tread:

Leader: Lord, in your mercy
All: Forgive us.

When we fail to hear your
  gentle word,
choosing other voices
to follow instead:

Leader: Lord, in your mercy
All: Forgive us.

When we hesitate to speak
  your name,
fearful of our failings
or of what might be said:

Leader: Lord, in your mercy
All: Forgive us.

Thanksgiving

We give thanks
that even within the bustle
of Christmas shopping
and consumerism,
an echo of the truth
can be discerned
in celebration,
carols being sung
and the offering of gifts.

Thank you for opportunities
to point the way
through shopping mall,
Christmas trees
and sparkling lights,
to the shepherds,
  a stable,
and, in deep humility,
a Saviour's birth.

Fourth Sunday of Advent

Sunday between 18 and 24 December

2 SAMUEL 7:1–11, 16; PSALM 89:1–4, 19–26; LUKE 1:46–55; ROMANS 16:25–27;
LUKE 1:26–38

Opening prayer

Through our worship today,
bring us ever nearer,
in our Advent journeying,
to Bethlehem's stable,
expectation
and celebration.

Adoration

We will sing of your love
  for ever,
and proclaim your faithfulness
to every generation,
for your word is dependable,
your promises secure.

A child is to be born
within one nation
but for all nations.
Our God will be revealed,
the Son of David
born in humility.
Love will come down to earth
as servant-king
and vulnerable.

We will sing of your love
  for ever,
and proclaim your faithfulness
to every generation,
for by grace incomparable
our salvation is here.

Confession

As we celebrate
the gift of love
within a manger
and remember
that Jesus Christ
came for our salvation,
forgive us
if our hearts are cold
and faith is hard to find.

Bring us back to the mother,
Mary, who bore the child
who would be king.
Remind us of her
gentleness,
her faithfulness
when asked to be
the blessed one
through whom
the divine would walk
upon this earth.
Oh, that we should
  demonstrate
such faith!

Thanksgiving

When you come to us
with gentle whisper
or mighty wind,
and ask what seems impossible
to human minds,
as you did with Mary,
may our response
not be to hesitate,
make excuses
or run away,
but to echo instead
those trusting
and beautiful words,
'I am the Lord's servant;
may your word be fulfilled
  in me.'

For Mary's faithfulness
and her life of service
we thank you, Lord.

Christmas Day

ISAIAH 52:7–10; PSALM 98; HEBREWS 1:1–4 [5–12]; JOHN 1:1–14

Opening prayer

We are here
to bring good tidings
of great joy,
and to proclaim
that in the birth of the
  Christ-child
and the humility of a
  stable
is God's salvation
for every nation upon
  earth.

Adoration

Leader: Sing to the Lord a new song
**All: For he has done marvellous
  things.**

Through prophets' words
and angel voices
the Lord has made his will known
for the salvation of the world.

Leader: Sing to the Lord a new song
**All: For he has done marvellous
  things.**

Through priest and king
and faithful service
the Lord has kept his promise
to those who he calls his children.

Leader: Sing to the Lord a new song
**All: For he has done marvellous
  things.**

Through Christ, all things
beneath the heavens
were brought into existence;
now the divine steps down to earth.

Leader: Sing to the Lord a new song
**All: For he has done marvellous
  things.**

Confession

In a humble stable,
ignored by all
within Bethlehem's walls,
the divine touched this earth,
breathed the air we breathe
and walked the ground we
  walk.
Born to sacrifice;
born to bring us life.

Forgive our reluctance
to proclaim this to the world;
forgive our ingratitude
when we disregard your word.
Bring us to that place
where shepherds heard
the angels sing,
and send us out
to share that glorious song.

Thanksgiving

For the brightness
of Bethlehem's star,
announcing
to all who can see
that a Saviour is to be born,
we give you thanks.

For the beauty
of the angels' song,
announcing
to all who can hear
that the time is drawing near,
we give you thanks.

For the pure joy
of a mother's cry,
announcing
God's blessing on her
with such faith and humility,
we give you thanks.

First Sunday of Christmas

Sunday between 26 December and 1 January

ISAIAH 61:10—62:3; PSALM 148; GALATIANS 4:4–7; LUKE 2:22–40

Opening prayer

We join with creation
and the angels above
in praising our maker
and redeemer
for the wonders around us,
the glory of his grace,
and the Christ-child,
born in a stable
who is salvation
for all people upon earth.

Adoration

It is your name
that we exalt above all others,
your glory
that we lift up in worship—
you who set the planets in
   motion
and illuminate the heavens
by day and night;
you whose endless love for
   creation
caused you to walk upon this
   earth
as Prince of Peace
and Servant-king.

Praise him, angels above!
Praise him, saints below!
Join the heavenly chorus
and praise the Lord!

Confession

You have brought us into your
  family,
no longer slaves to sin
but precious children
loved by a heavenly Father,
saved by your Son, our
  Saviour.

When we forget our spiritual
  heritage,
your saints of every age
who faithfully lived and died
to spread this good news,
  forgive us.

When our hearts are cold and
  we are tempted
to walk a different path
or deny the truth we have
  been told,
bring us back to the stable;
remind us of the day love came
  to earth.

Thanksgiving

Love comes to us
fragile as a tiny seed,
which can
germinate and grow
into the tallest of trees,
or wither and die
if left carelessly around.

Love comes to us
fragile as a tiny child,
who is
salvation and grace
for sinners wanting release,
or judgement for hearts
offering just stony ground.

Love comes to us—
and to the stable
we now journey,
bringing precious gifts
as an offering to our
Saviour and King,
the sweet-smelling fragrance
of our thanksgiving.

Second Sunday of Christmas

Sunday between 2 and 5 January

JEREMIAH 31:7–14; PSALM 147:12–20; EPHESIANS 1:3–14; JOHN 1:[1–9] 10–18

Opening prayer

We meet today
as children of the living God,
through his glorious grace
and our Saviour, Jesus Christ.
We raise our voices
in worship and praise
for all that he has done
and will do,
in this place and in these lives.

Adoration

God who made us,
who has always known us
and placed his mark upon us,
we praise your holy name.

God who saves us,
who became flesh for us
and was sacrificed for us,
we praise your holy name.

God who empowers us,
who breathes life within us
and daily sustains us,
we praise your holy name.

Holy and blessed Trinity,
oneness that binds us
and presence around us,
we praise your holy name.

Confession

When we fail to see
the peace of Christ
in a word of comfort spoken
or an arm around our
  shoulder,
forgive us.

When we fail to see
the love of Christ
in the sharing of a burden
or the actions of a stranger,
forgive us.

Open our eyes to see
your love revealed,
and open our hearts
in gratitude
and service,
that through our lives
others might glimpse
a spark of the divine.

Thanksgiving

Leader: Thanks be to the Lord
**All: Who is worthy of our
  praise.**

For grace beyond imagining,
that takes the very least of us
and offers full salvation:

Leader: Thanks be to the Lord
**All: Who is worthy of our
  praise.**

For love that's everlasting
and, from the very dawn of
  time,
has marked us out as precious:

Leader: Thanks be to the Lord
**All: Who is worthy of our
  praise.**

For joy that is our blessing
and a gift that's meant for
  sharing
with those who do not know
  him:

Leader: Thanks be to the Lord
**All: Who is worthy of our
  praise.**

The Epiphany

6 January or first Sunday in January

ISAIAH 60:1–6; PSALM 72:[1–7] 10–14; EPHESIANS 3:1–12; MATTHEW 2:1–12

Opening prayer

As wise men from the east
discovered the Christ-child
and offered their precious gifts,
so we gather today
to bring our offerings
of praise and service
to our Lord and Saviour.

Adoration

Your light
reveals to us
the beauty of this world,
for we see it through your eyes
and the purpose
for which it was created.

Your light
reveals to us
the darkness in this world,
for we see things as they are
and how your children,
once lost, might be set free.

Your light
reveals to us
the wonder of your grace,
for we see within your Son
the hope of salvation
and, through him, new life.

Confession

When your light shines
on those in need
through hunger,
injustice,
oppression or fear,
and we stay silent,
wash our hands
and carry on,
forgive us.

You came to earth
for such as these,
fed the hungry,
healed the sick,
conquered fear,
spoke out,
turned over tables,
challenged the way things
  were,
and then passed the torch
into the hands of your
  disciples.

Grant us the courage,
compassion and faith
to shine your light
into unfamiliar
and less comfortable places.

Thanksgiving

The magi followed a star
on a long and arduous journey
to the place where Jesus lay,
while shepherds were back in
  their fields,
the town's many visitors were
  gone
and life was almost back to
  normal,
but for the presence
of the long-hoped-for
  Messiah—
a precious child
ignored by most who passed by
within Bethlehem's narrow
  streets.

For all who have journeyed
and found their Saviour,
we give you thanks, and pray
that those who have silently
  passed by
might one day return
and find the one
who has waited patiently for
  them.

Baptism of Christ

Sunday between 7 and 13 January
GENESIS 1:1–5; PSALM 29; ACTS 19:1–7; MARK 1:4–11

Opening prayer

We worship you,
O Lord our God,
in the splendour of your
  holiness,
in full knowledge of your grace
  and mercy
and in the presence of your
  people,
our brothers and sisters in
  Christ.
We worship you,
O Lord our God.

Adoration

In the beginning
you were there,
and this world
and all within it
were part of your creative plan.

In the beginning
you were there,
Father, Son
and Holy Spirit,
with eternity in your hands.

In the beginning
you were there,
Creator,
and your word brought light
to a dark and barren land.

Confession

Remind us, Lord,
as we struggle
with the burdens of this life,
that when you walked
from the baptismal
waters of the Jordan,
you submitted to a life
of divine service and sacrifice.

Blind would see,
deaf hear,
lame would leap for joy—
and for our sake,
those not even born,
you suffered
humiliation,
arms outstretched
in love
upon a cross.

It puts our burdens
into perspective, Lord.
Forgive us, remind us
and encircle us
in those loving arms, we pray.

Thanksgiving

For those who,
through word and deed,
proclaim your name
within these streets,
who live the life they preach
and, by the Spirit, testify
to the one who has
and is to come;
for those who have led us
us to the place
where longings can be satisfied
by the one who is
truly Son of God,
we are truly thankful.
Bless them,
and may their example
be the inspiration for our lives.

Second Sunday of Epiphany

Sunday between 14 and 20 January

1 SAMUEL 3:1–10 [11–20]; PSALM 139:1–6, 13–18; 1 CORINTHIANS 6:12–20; JOHN 1:43–51

Opening prayer

You speak to us in many ways:
in the quiet of our worship,
the singing of our hymns,
the reading of your word,
the fellowship we share.
Open our ears and hearts
that we might hear your gentle
  voice
and, hearing, respond.

Adoration

You know us
and yet call us,
imperfect though we are,
to be your light in this world,
to bring wholeness and release,
heal the sick,
support the weak.
You know us,
and yet call us
to be vessels of your grace.

That you should trust us with
  this mission
is too difficult to grasp,
and the task,
in our strength,
is impossible.
You know us,
  call us,
    use us,
but more importantly
by your Spirit
empower us.

Confession

Sometimes, Lord,
we forget that you have
  welcomed us
into your kingdom,
and prefer to walk within a
  world
that daily tempts us.

Sometimes, Lord,
we forget the freedom given us
in your kingdom,
and prefer the shackles that we
  knew
before you called us.

Remind us, Lord,
of the price you paid so we can
  enter
into your kingdom.
Forgive, and accept our
  gratitude
for such grace shown to us.

Thanksgiving

Leader: We give thanks for
  your call
All: And we will follow
Leader: To be your witnesses
and bring the light of Christ
into this world.

Leader: We give thanks for
  your call
All: And we will follow
Leader: To where you lead us,
for you will keep us safe
within your arms.

Leader: We give thanks for
  your call
All: And we will follow
Leader: To be a powerful voice
where there is injustice
and suffering.

Leader: We give thanks for
  your call
All: And we will follow
Leader: To show your love and
  grace
in our lives as our
thanks-living offering.

Third Sunday of Epiphany

Sunday between 21 and 27 January

JONAH 3:1–5, 10; PSALM 62:5–12; 1 CORINTHIANS 7:29–31; MARK 1:14–20

Opening prayer

We set aside this time,
precious moments
in the presence of
Father, Son and Spirit,
Holy Trinity.
May we be blessed
and become a blessing,
and may our prayers
be a fragrant offering
to you, O Lord our God.

Adoration

You are the rock
on which we build,
a sure foundation
that will not move.
You are a fortress,
dependable,
a secure refuge
none can destroy.

In you we trust
to keep us safe;
all other ground
is sinking sand.
In you we live,
for all we are
and hope to be
is in your hand.

Confession

Your call to us
does not end
with an invitation
to become your disciples
but continues
in our daily walk
as we hear your gentle whisper
and simply stop to listen.

But listening
can be hard
when the cry of this world
is so insistent.
So forgive us, we pray.
Give us ears
to hear this world
and heaven's voice,
and wisdom
to know the difference.

Thanksgiving

Thank you for your love,
patient and kind,
slow to anger,
full of grace
and mercy,
for it warmed these hearts,
sometimes made cold
by neglect or circumstance.

Thank you for love's
transforming power,
moulding us into the people
you would have us be—
confident of faith,
willing for service
and united in our desire
that all might respond
to the knowledge
of your redeeming love.

Fourth Sunday of Epiphany

Sunday between 28 January and 3 February

DEUTERONOMY 18:15–20; PSALM 111; 1 CORINTHIANS 8:1–13; MARK 1:21–28

Opening prayer

In this place and at this time,
as we gather in your name,
be the peace that we desire,
the healing that we seek,
the forgiveness that we need,
in this place and at this time,
as we gather in your name.

Adoration

To know you
is to love you, Lord,
for your glory
and majesty
are visible to all
who have eyes to see
and hearts to appreciate;
your faithfulness
and salvation
are offered to all
who fall to their knees
in need of grace and mercy.
To know you
is to love you, Lord.

Confession

Heavenly Father,
you have brought us
from wilderness
to promised land,
provided for us, blessed us
and protected us from harm.

Forgive our reluctance
to speak your name,
share your grace
and be the means
by which you touch
lives that are in need.
Use, we pray, these hands,
these feet, these voices
to bring your blessing
to all we meet.

Thanksgiving

In a world of
uncertainties,
where people are
questioning,
seeking answers,
searching for
a purpose in life,
this one thing
is certain and true—
that you are God,
and heaven
  and earth
and everything
  within
were created
by your hand.

We thank you, Creator God,
that the answer
to their questions
is found in you.

Proper 1

Sunday between 4 and 10 February
(if earlier than Second Sunday before Lent)

ISAIAH 40:21–31; PSALM 147:1–11, 20C; 1 CORINTHIANS 9:16–23; MARK 1:29–39

Opening prayer

This is your new day,
and we praise you
for the opportunities
it provides
for prayer
and worship,
teaching
and insight,
sharing
and service.
This is your new day,
and we praise you.

Adoration

In the rising and setting
of the sun each day
you remind us
that, within a changing
and confusing world,
there is a constancy
we can depend upon.
Your creative breath
that set this universe in motion
still breathes upon it now,
dispelling darkness,
bringing dawn
and hope to those
who have eyes of faith,
that see beyond the ordinary
to a glorious you!

Confession

Lord Jesus,
you walked this earth
as friend of the vulnerable,
defender of the weak,
bringing wholeness
to lives that were broken,
healing to the sick.

As for us,
who tread our streets
as if walking in your footsteps
but looking through our eyes,
grant forgiveness
for those we have passed by
rather than assisted.

Remind us
who meet today
that our call is not just to
  follow
but to have hearts that reach
  out
where there is need,
bringing your love and grace
into this fragile world.

Thanksgiving

Thank you for all those
who have, by their example,
inspired us to greater things
than we could have imagined,
who have walked that extra
  mile
with you and demonstrated
that all things are possible
for those who put their trust
  in you.

Bless their endeavours and all
whose lives have been touched
by their faithfulness.
We ask this through Jesus
  Christ,
who gave everything,
that we might know
the true value of all things.

Proper 2

Sunday between 11 and 17 February
(if earlier than Second Sunday before Lent)

2 KINGS 5:1–14; PSALM 30; 1 CORINTHIANS 9:24–27; MARK 1:40–45

Opening prayer

Bless all who are gathered
for worship here today.
Bless those who lead
and those who serve.
Bless those who are strong
and those who are weak.
Bless those who are young
and those who are old.
Bless all who are gathered
for worship here today.

Adoration

You come to us
in unexpected ways,
bringing healing,
wholeness
and restoration
of body, mind and soul.
Not in burning bush,
lightning flash
or thunder's roar,
but in quiet word,
gentleness
and healing touch.

May our hearts reveal
a willingness to
embrace quietness,
hear your whisper
and understand more
of your love,
grace and truth.

Confession

To you alone we come,
Saviour,
Redeemer,
Priest and King,
trusting in your grace
and willingness to forgive.
To you alone we come,
  weighed down
with the burden of our sin,
  captive,
asking only for release.

To you alone we come,
Saviour,
Redeemer,
Priest and King,
that our hearts might
be moved to service
and not be still.

Thanksgiving

When hearts are heavy,
bodies weak,
lives filled with sadness,
spirits low;
when days are lonely,
dark with cloud,
preventing sunshine
breaking through;
thank you for the assurance
that you are
never further away
than a whispered prayer
can reach,
never closer
than when we're weary
and on our knees.

Year B

Proper 3

Sunday between 18 and 24 February
(if earlier than Second Sunday before Lent)
ISAIAH 43:18–25; PSALM 41; 2 CORINTHIANS 1:18–22; MARK 2:1–12

Opening prayer

For freedom of worship,
meeting openly in your name,
we thank you, Lord.
For those meeting in secret
in fear of arrest
and those whose commitment
might cost them their life,
for all who are gathering
for worship today,
we ask your blessing, Lord.

Adoration

God of new beginnings,
you take
the raw material
of our lives
and transform us
through your Spirit
into the people
we were intended to be,
for the glory of your name.

God of new beginnings,
you bring
within the wilderness
of our lives
living water
to sustain us
in our walk with you,
and, nourished by your Spirit,
we shall glorify your name.

Confession

When faith is weak
and can't sustain us,
  be close;
strengthen
and bless us, we pray.

When temptation
has its hold on us,
  forgive,
restore,
empower us, we pray.

When we fail to
recognise your voice,
  whisper
once more
into our hearts, we pray.

May we become
witnesses for you,
  faithful,
sure and
confident, today.

Thanksgiving

On you, O Lord,
we can depend,
for your promises
throughout history
have been fulfilled
in Christ Jesus,
who lived,
  walked
    and died
upon this earth,
that we might understand
your faithfulness
and, by the cross
and glorious resurrection,
know within our hearts
the reality of your love
for each one of us.

And so we join
with all your children,
wherever they might be,
affirming our thanksgiving
in one glorious 'Amen'.

Second Sunday before Lent

HOSEA 2:14–20; PSALM 103:1–13, 22; 2 CORINTHIANS 3:1–6; MARK 2:13–22

Opening prayer

As we join together in worship,
we remember those
who would love to be with us
but are prevented—
those who are unwell,
those on holiday,
those who are infirm.
Join us in spirit and bless
   them,
as you bless us, with your
   presence.

Adoration

In the beginning, Lord,
before all things,
you were—
light and life,
word and truth
revealed yet misunderstood
within the darkness of this
   world.

In your time, Lord,
you came,
born to this earth
to draw all who might
believe in your name
into the family of a living God.

In your time, Lord,
all creation
will see your light,
kneel at your feet
and acknowledge you as Lord.
For as high as the stars
are above this earth,
so great is your love for us.

Confession

God of compassion,
we open our hearts to you,
laying bare that of which
we are ashamed,
the visible scars
and self-inflicted wounds
that weaken our faith and
  service.
We ask for your forgiveness,
and for reconciliation
where we have caused
pain or distress.

God of compassion,
forgive and restore, we pray,
through the one who took
  our sin
upon his broad shoulders
and died that we might know
the true cost of your love
  for us.

Thanksgiving

For your Spirit,
which gives life
to these dry bones,
we thank you.

For your love,
which softens
a heart of stone,
we thank you.

For your word,
which directs
the path we tread,
we thank you.

For your grace
and gospel,
the truth we spread,
we thank you.

Year B

Sunday Next before Lent

2 KINGS 2:1–12; PSALM 50:1–6; 2 CORINTHIANS 4:3–6; MARK 9:2–9

Opening prayer

Throughout the world,
your people
are worshipping,
in cathedral and chapel,
hidden rooms,
prison cells,
together,
alone.
In this place
and throughout the world,
praises are rising
as a fragrant offering
to our Saviour and Lord.

Adoration

What does this world need?
To know this—
that we are loved
and cherished,
of great worth,
unique and precious.

What does this world need?
To know this—
that the God who made light
shine into darkness
lets his light shine in human
  hearts,
so we might know him
and see his glory displayed
in the face of Christ Jesus.

What does this world need?
To know this, and only this—
that we are loved by God.

Confession

You come to us as
Saviour, Shepherd,
Prince of Peace, Son of God.
This world sees you
as teacher, wise man,
enlightened, rebel.

If we have failed
to share the truth
of who you are,
forgive us.
May the world
hear once again,
through our words
or through revelation,
the Father's glorious words
break through the clouds
surrounding them:
'This is my Son, whom I love.
Listen to him!'

Thanksgiving

Thank you, Lord,
for those mountaintop
  experiences
when you seem so close
your voice clear,
our faith strong.

Thank you for those precious
  moments
when we can put aside
that which hurts us,
tempts us
or distracts us.

We rest within the glorious
  presence
of your company,
before descending
to the valley floor,
that holy place
where we walk each day.
Be as close to us there
as you are
on the mountaintop,
and bless this day to us,
O Lord, we pray.

Year B

First Sunday of Lent

GENESIS 9:8–17; PSALM 25:1–10; 1 PETER 3:18–22; MARK 1:9–15

Opening prayer

In our meeting for worship,
bless the joining of these lives
and the fellowship it provides.
As we leave this sacred space,
may the blessing we receive
be the blessing that we give,
through Jesus Christ alone,
　we pray.

Adoration

After the storm
a rainbow,
our glorious reminder
of covenant
between Creator
and creation,
God's loving arms
encircling the world.

After the storm
a rainbow,
our glorious reminder
of gracious love
between Father
and children,
God's loving arms
encircling our worship.

Confession

In you alone, O Lord,
do we place our trust.
When we were wandering
on rough and stony ground,
you reached out, lifted
and brought us safely home,
our good shepherd
gently caring for his sheep.

We are still prone to wander
from the path you place us on,
eyes easily distracted,
listening to a different song,
still tempted
by the waywardness of youth.
Now we humbly ask
for your forgiveness
and the encircling of your love
to keep us safe from harm.
For in you alone, O Lord,
do we place our trust.

Thanksgiving

Lord, you do not give up
  on us,
even when we wander;
you guide us in your truth,
illuminating a path
that we can safely follow.

You do not give up on us
even though we fail you;
you bless us
as love, so amazing,
pours in and through our
  hearts
in a constant stream of grace.

You do not give up on us;
in you alone we trust,
and, gathered here today,
we bring this grateful offering
of praise and thankfulness.

Second Sunday of Lent

GENESIS 17:1–7, 15–16; PSALM 22:23–31; ROMANS 4:13–25; MARK 8:31–38

Opening prayer

God of love,
be the love that we find here
and share with friend and
    stranger.

God of peace,
be the peace that we find here
and share with friend and
    stranger.

God of joy,
be the joy that we find here
and share with friend and
    stranger.

Adoration

Creator of a universe
beyond imagining,
yet close enough
to hear
a whispered prayer
and hold
an outstretched hand—
this is our God.

We join a heavenly chorus
joyfully declaring
that those who seek
    will find
and those who find
    will know
such love and grace,
beyond imagining.
This is our God.

Confession

You willingly walked
the path laid out for you,
striding purposefully
toward Jerusalem
and a crowd
that one moment
welcomed
and then cried,
'Crucify!'

Forgive us
who hesitate
along the road,
when our stride shortens
and our faith is challenged
as we glance
toward the cross.
Grant us courage
and perseverance
in our journeying with you,
for we cannot do it
in our strength alone.

Thanksgiving

By faith we know
you created us
for a purpose,
love us
unconditionally,
call us
to follow you,
forgive us
when we fail you,
raise us up
when we stumble,
and bless us
in your service.

Receive our grateful thanks
that your promises
are always true,
and your faithfulness
can be relied on
eternally.

Third Sunday of Lent

EXODUS 20:1–17; PSALM 19; 1 CORINTHIANS 1:18–25; JOHN 2:13–22

Opening prayer

Heavenly Father,
in your name we gather,
young, old,
  rich, poor,
    local
or travelling far.
In your name we gather,
and in your name we are
brother,
  sister,
    family,
in the presence of our
heavenly Father.

Adoration

Earth joins heaven in declaring
your glory, Creator God.
No words are spoken,
no song is sung,
but in the solitude
of mountaintop
or setting sun
their voice can be heard
above the murmurs of this
  world.
Such beauty,
  such provision,
    such knowledge
dispel the mists of doubt,
until our hearts are joined in
  the one
who is the source of all,
and we are drawn to worship.

Confession

Forgive us, Lord,
who call ourselves your own
but daily cause you pain,
who see someone in need
and walk across the road,
hear about injustice
and fail to say a word.

Forgive us, Lord,
who call ourselves your own.
Renew our hearts,
our souls and minds;
strengthen our faith
and make us a people
of whom you can be proud,
who are your hands,
your feet and voice within this
  world.

Thanksgiving

God of wholeness,
God of grace,
to you we bring our thanks
  and praise.

To a world that searches,
you are a lamp that shines;
to a world that is hungry,
you are food that sustains;
to a world that suffers,
you are hope of release;
to a world that's broken,
you are one who restores;
to a world full of hate,
you are love that forgives;
to a world that denies,
you are truth that endures.

To you we bring our thanks
  and praise,
God of wholeness,
God of grace.

Fourth Sunday of Lent

NUMBERS 21:4–9; PSALM 107:1–3, 17–22; EPHESIANS 2:1–10; JOHN 3:14–21

Opening prayer

Bless those of us meeting for
  worship
and those who would be here
if circumstance did not keep us
  apart.
Bring comfort to the lonely,
  healing to the sick
and, in due course, join us
  together
once more, to enjoy sweet
  fellowship
and worship you, our Lord
  and God.

Adoration

Leader: O worship the Lord,
  for he is good.
All: His love endures for ever.

He set this world in motion
and engineers each turn;
he gave to us such beauty,
both seen and still unseen.

Leader: O worship the Lord,
  for he is good.
All: His love endures for ever.

He shepherded a nation,
and from captivity
created new beginnings
from that which once had been.

Leader: O worship the Lord,
  for he is good.
All: His love endures for ever.

He loves us with a passion
that draws us back to him
and by the cross he bridges
the chasm of our sin.

Leader: O worship the Lord,
  for he is good.
All: His love endures for ever.

Confession

When impatience is a cause of
  stress
on our journeying with you,
and the wanting to be
  somewhere else
spoils our enjoyment of the
  view,
forgive us,
and draw us close again,
we pray.

When circumstance produces
  doubt
and we drift away from you,
or the wisdom of the world
  pulls us
away from that we know is
  true,
forgive us,
and draw us close again,
we pray.

Thanksgiving

Thank you, Lord,
that when we are feeling
  proud,
    arrogant,
beyond reproach,
pleased with ourselves,
self-sufficient in our ways,
you remind us
that, for people like us
and all of humankind,
you sent your Son into the
  world,
to save us from ourselves
before we stumble,
  fall
    and are hurt.

Thank you, Lord, that you
  embrace us
and enable us
to become the people
we were always meant to be—
children of a loving Father,
blessing others through
  your love.

Fifth Sunday in Lent

JEREMIAH 31:31–34; PSALM 51:1–12; HEBREWS 5:5–10; JOHN 12:20–33

Opening prayer

In this time of worship
we bring to you
the offering of our praise,
the opening of our hearts
and the service of our lives,
that in this place
your name might be heard
and lifted high.

Adoration

Inscribed upon our heart,
the maker's mark,
indelible,
the word of God.
  'Love'
beautifully written,
  heartfelt,
that all God's people
  might know
that we are precious,
  children
of a heavenly Father
becoming family together.
May our eyes lift upward
as we listen together
to hear angels worship.

Confession

When our lives do not reflect
the light that is within,
and by word,
　action
　　or inaction
we cause you sorrow,
failing to become
along our daily walk
your voice,
　your hands
　　or feet,
forgive us, gracious God.

Revive again the fire once lit
within our hearts
and grant once more a love
that overflows with you.

Thanksgiving

If your name is preached
or in conversation
discussed,
a seed is sown
that may in due course
germinate,
　grow
　　and blossom
in the fertile ground
of a receptive heart.

For those who sow,
whether on well-tilled soil
or barren ground,
and for the lives
which now bear fruit
from that faithful service,
we give our grateful thanks.

Palm Sunday

LITURGY OF THE PALMS: PSALM 118:1–2, 19–29; MARK 11:1–11; JOHN 12:12–16

LITURGY OF THE PASSION: ISAIAH 50:4–9A; PSALM 31:9–16; PHILIPPIANS 2:5–11; MARK 14:1—15:47

Opening prayer

We join with the voices of
  those
who stood and cheered
as Jesus entered Jerusalem,
laying not palm branches
but our lives down at his feet.
'Hosanna!
Blessed is he who comes
in the name of the Lord!
Hosanna in the highest
  heaven!'

Adoration

The road you chose,
that led to Jerusalem,
was not an easy one
but it was a necessary journey,
from humble birth
to a shameful death—
exalted,
  rejected,
the eternal mystery
of the cross.

There are other roads,
built by human hands,
that offer temporary comforts,
but only this one
has its destination
in the heart of God,
and only this one
is safe for us to follow.

Confession

How quickly cries
of 'Hosanna!'
turn to 'Crucify!'
when Jesus refuses
to be moulded into that
which we would have
 him be.

Forgive us, dear Lord,
who sing 'Hosanna!'
as you draw near,
yet in our daily lives
reveal ourselves no better
than those who caused your
 pain.

May this be the song
of our hearts this passiontide,
as we lay our lives before
 you:
'Hosanna! Blessed is he
who comes in the name of
 the Lord!
Hosanna in the highest!'

Thanksgiving

Leader: To you, O Lord, we lift
 our hearts
All: In gratitude and praise.

Your love is eternal;
from generation to generation
you have cared and provided
for those who call on your name.

Leader: To you, O Lord, we lift
 our hearts
All: In gratitude and praise.

Your love is merciful;
from generation to generation
you have loved and forgiven
those who humbly turn to you.

Leader: To you, O Lord, we lift
 our hearts
All: In gratitude and praise.

Your love is empowering;
from generation to generation
you have blessed with your Spirit
those who give their lives to you.

Leader: To you, O Lord, we lift
 our hearts
All: In gratitude and praise.

Good Friday

ISAIAH 52:12—53:12; PSALM 22; HEBREWS 10:16–25 [HEBREWS 4:14–16; 5:7–9]; JOHN 18:1—19:42

Opening prayer

A few moments of quiet at the start of our worship enable us to think about the day that we are commemorating. The journey to Jerusalem and Palm Sunday are in the past... *(Pause)*

Now there are cruelty, injustice, rejection and a cruel cross... *(Pause)*

Now there is also the willing sacrifice of Jesus Christ, dying for all who have rejected and always will always reject him, along with the whole of humanity... *(Pause)*

Gracious God, be with us and speak through the scriptures and hymns we sing, that we might begin to understand the reality of the day we call Good Friday.

Adoration

Love did not die
upon the cross
but, arms outstretched,
still welcomes us,
the twisted thorns
bejewelled with
pearls of blood—
a fitting crown
for the one who is
the servant-king,
leading his people
victorious through
death's dark vale
into a promised land.

Love did not die
upon the cross
but, arms outstretched,
still welcomes us.

Confession

Each time
we do not speak your name
for fear of ridicule,
we deny you.

Each time
we do not bring your love
into a situation,
we deny you.

Each time
we fail to see your face
in friend or stranger,
we deny you.

Forgive us,
as you forgive all
who humbly turn to you,
and open our eyes once more
to the reality of the cross.

Thanksgiving

God of love,
in a moment of quiet
we remember
the love that brought us
to this place.

(Silence)

God of love,
in a moment of quiet
we remember
the arms outstretched
in our place.

(Silence)

God of love,
in a moment of quiet
we bring our grateful thanks.

(Silence)

Year B

Easter Day

ACTS 10:34–43; PSALM 118:1–2, 14–24; 1 CORINTHIANS 15:1–11; JOHN 20:1–18

Opening prayer

To a sceptical world
that would trust
in human wisdom alone,
we are here today
to testify in our worship
that Jesus Christ,
once crucified,
is risen from the grave
and is with us as we pray.

Adoration

Rejoice!
The stone is rolled away,
and Jesus Christ
is risen from the grave.
Hallelujah!

Rejoice!
Love is victorious;
the Son of God
holds out his hands for us.
Hallelujah!

Rejoice!
For sin no longer has
a hold on us;
through grace we are set free.
Hallelujah!

Confession

Would we be counted
among the doubters,
hiding in the shadow
cast by that cruel cross?
Or, when challenged,
like Peter
openly deny you?

There are times, Lord,
when doubts assail
and the distance between us
seems to increase.
There are times, Lord,
when sin has its hold,
like a barrier between us
that will not move.

Who is there we can turn to
when we feel so
  overwhelmed?
Who can roll away the stone
and reveal the empty tomb?
No one but you, Jesus,
no one but you.

Thanksgiving

Love poured out
on that cruel cross,
a blood-offering
so we might go free.
Thank you, Christ our Lord.

(Pause)

Love poured out,
infusing this world
with rivers of grace
and hope of rebirth.
Thank you, Christ our Lord.

(Pause)

Love poured out
and into our hearts;
we drink from a stream
that never runs dry.
Thank you, Christ our Lord.

Year B

Second Sunday of Easter

ACTS 4:32–35; PSALM 133; 1 JOHN 1:1—2:2; JOHN 20:19–31

Opening prayer

In the name of the Father,
who loved this universe
  into being,
we join together in worship.

In the name of the Son,
who died that we might know
  eternal life,
we join together in worship.

In the name of the Spirit,
whose flame burns brightly
  within our hearts,
we join together in worship.

Father, Son and Holy Spirit,
glorious Trinity, three in one,
it is you alone we worship.

Adoration

We have the message of Jesus
to proclaim to the world.

The Word of God,
eternal truth
confined within
frail human flesh.

The Son of God,
who for this world
poured out his love
upon the cross.

The light of life,
by whom we feel
the grace of God
setting us free.

We have the message of Jesus
to proclaim to the world.

Confession

It would be wrong, Lord,
for us to say that
we have no doubts,
for this world is trying
to deny all we hold dear,
and is insistent in its cry.
There are days when,
like Thomas, your dear friend,
we need to reach out
and touch the hand
that has led us these long
   years,
to see the place
where spear and nails
have made their marks.

Forgive our doubts
and, in times of temptation,
be our confidence,
so close that, like Thomas,
we might joyfully declare,
'My Lord and my God!'

Thanksgiving

The love you show
is our inspiration;
the light you give,
our illumination
along the path we walk
with you this day.

It is our witness to the world
to be of one mind
in heart and soul,
a blessing
to friend and stranger,
bringing your grace
to those in need
and good news
to the lost and the seeker.

For love, light
and all the blessings
of this life,
we offer our grateful thanks.

Third Sunday of Easter

ACTS 3:12–19; PSALM 4; 1 JOHN 3:1–7; LUKE 24:36B–48

Opening prayer

Thank you for this new day,
for the opportunity of meeting
in the safety of your house.
Bless those who meet in secret,
behind locked doors,
fearful of persecution or arrest.
May we never forget the
  suffering
so many have endured,
that we might know freedom
to worship freely in this place.

Adoration

What a blessing
you have lavished upon us,
that we can be known as
children of God.

What a treasure
you have presented to us,
with this pearl of great price,
the word of God.

What a privilege
you have bestowed upon us,
made citizens of the
kingdom of God.

What a harvest
you have prepared around us,
all who are seeking the
mercy of God.

Confession

Forgive us, Lord,
when doubts assail,
we miss your whisper,
stray from the path
or fail to see you
in friend or stranger.
Open our hearts and minds
to the understanding
of your word,
and grant us a faith
lived in the light
of your resurrection life.
Give us ears to hear you,
eyes to see you,
and feet to follow
wherever you might lead.

Thanksgiving

Leader: For all the blessings
that you give
**All: We offer our grateful
thanks.**

For light that shines within
our hearts
when all around is darkness;
for love that hears us when
we call
and answers our distress:

Leader: For all the blessings
that you give
**All: We offer our grateful
thanks.**

For joy that offers us such
warmth
when lives are under stress,
for peace that takes away
our fear
and brings to us sweet rest:

Leader: For all the blessings
that you give
**All: We offer our grateful
thanks.**

Fourth Sunday of Easter

ACTS 4:5–12; PSALM 23; 1 JOHN 3:16–24; JOHN 10:11–18

Opening prayer

This is your day,
gifted to us
as sabbath rest,
and we will rejoice in it.
Bring peace
to these busy lives,
and calm
our anxious hearts.
This is your day,
gifted to us
as sabbath rest,
and we will rejoice in it.

Adoration

What is love?
It is this,
that you, Creator God,
who set this universe in
  motion,
should care
for people like us.

What is love?
It is this,
that you, good shepherd,
who know each of your sheep,
should lay down your life
for people like us.

What is love?
It is this,
that we should follow
the example of Christ in this
  world
and love
all people like us.

Confession

You know us better
than we know ourselves—
our thoughts,
  our motives,
    our burdens.

Living water,
flow through these lives;
wash away all that hinders—
the past we cling to,
the accumulated debris
of our daily lives.
Cleanse,
  refresh,
    revive.

Make us fit for service,
that we might be
your hands,
  your feet,
    your words,
wherever you might need us.

Thanksgiving

On this, our journey of faith,
we trust in you alone,
  Good Shepherd,
guiding us
  along a path you are familiar
  with;
leading us
  beside green pastures and
  quiet waters;
feeding us
  with your word as
  refreshment for our souls;
steering us
  from that which might tempt
  and divert;
protecting us
  from that which might harm
  or destroy.

We trust in you alone, Good
  Shepherd,
on this, our journey of faith,
and we thank you for your
  constant care.

Fifth Sunday of Easter

ACTS 8:26–40; PSALM 22:25–31; 1 JOHN 4:7–21; JOHN 15:1–8

Opening prayer

On our walk with you,
we rest for a while,
listen
and worship,
for you are
the one who guides us,
the one who feeds us,
the one who blesses us
and the one who keeps us safe.
On our walk with you,
we rest for a while,
listen
and worship.

Adoration

With your love in our hearts,
these branches of your vine
blossom and bear a fruitful
    crop,
nourished by the bread of life,
refreshed by living water,
nurtured by your gracious
    hand.

With your love in our hearts,
these branches of your vine
can spread the sweet perfume
of your blessing to this world
and draw others to your feet
in grateful praise and worship.

Confession

Forgive our need
to be in control,
the agenda for each day
written by our hands,
each moment mapped out
and presented,
fully formed.

Grant us confidence
to let go, be free
and available,
to follow where you lead,
into new challenges
and opportunities,
each day lived out
in humble service,
gratitude and faith.

Thanksgiving

Thank you, gracious Lord,
that you reveal yourself
to those who seek,
not always
in special places
   or sacred spaces,
but wherever we might be
on our daily journeying,
at work or play,
   night or day.

You take a seed of faith
that once was scattered
and unlock its potential,
allowing it to grow
   and blossom
within our grateful hearts.
To those who seek
you reveal yourself;
thank you, gracious Lord.

Sixth Sunday of Easter

ACTS 10:44–48; PSALM 98; 1 JOHN 5:1–6; JOHN 15:9–17

Opening prayer

We meet in your name,
your children
faithfully
worshipping
our heavenly Father.
Bless us now
in these quiet moments,
as you listen
to the prayers in our hearts.
May it be
precious time,
sacred time.

(Pause for reflection)

Adoration

This world has heard
the gospel message
through the witness
of generations
who lived,
shared
and breathed your word.

We are here today
because our hearts
were strangely warmed
by such an encounter,
and we believed,
as many did before,
that in Christ
and Christ alone
is our salvation.

For the Gospel message
and faithful witness,
we praise your name.

Confession

We have heard your voice
breaking through
the clutter of our lives,
calling us to share
the good news of Easter,
and have failed
to heed this simple call,
preferring to keep
this good news to ourselves.

God of mercy, forgive us,
open our ears to your voice
and stir our hearts into action.
Ignite the spark of faith
that still lies within,
that our lives might shine
with your radiance,
and your glory
be seen throughout the world.

Thanksgiving

God calls us chosen,
chosen to bear fruit
that will last.

Leader: God who calls us
All: We give you thanks.

God gives instruction,
instruction to love
as Christ loved.

Leader: God who calls us
All: We give you thanks.

God calls us to rest,
rest in that love
and be blessed.

Leader: God who calls us
All: We give you thanks.

God fills hearts with joy,
joy that inspires,
and builds up faith.

Leader: God who calls us
All: We give you thanks.

Ascension Day

May also be used on the Seventh Sunday of Easter

ACTS 1:1–11; PSALM 47; EPHESIANS 1:15–23; LUKE 24:44–53

Opening prayer

Gracious Father,
may our eyes be opened
to the riches
of our glorious inheritance,
and, through the power of the
  risen Christ,
may we know the hope to
  which we have been called,
and the blessings
of being a member of your
  family here on earth.

Adoration

Sing to the Lord
with songs of joy,
for he has saved his people
from the consequence of sin
and, through the cross and
  resurrection,
demonstrated his love and
  power.

Sing to the Lord
with songs of joy,
for he has kept his promise
and, by the Holy Spirit,
empowered his children to
  witness
here and to the ends of the
  earth.

Sing to the Lord
with songs of joy,
for he has prepared a place
within his glorious kingdom
for all who are called
by our risen and ascended
  Saviour,
Jesus Christ.

Confession

There are times, Lord,
when you seem far from us,
and the path we are walking
only takes us further
from where we ought to be.
Forgive our wandering spirit,
  Lord;
join us on this Emmaus road
and open up our minds
to the reality
of resurrection,
ascension
and the truth of who you are.

When we distance ourselves
from your presence,
in your mercy remind us
that you are closer
than we can ever imagine,
never further away
than a heart reaching out
or a whispered prayer.

Thanksgiving

Leader: Risen, ascended Lord
**All: Thank you for opening our
  eyes to you.**

You reveal yourself
in many ways
to those who seek your grace,
and in those encounters
on faith's journey
you point toward the truth
of cross and resurrection.

Leader: Risen, ascended Lord
**All: Thank you for opening our
  eyes to you.**

You reveal yourself
in many ways
to those who hear your voice,
and in those conversations
on faith's journey
you point the way toward
a glorious destination.

Leader: Risen, ascended Lord
**All: Thank you for opening our
  eyes to you.**

Seventh Sunday of Easter

ACTS 1:15–17, 21–26; PSALM 1; 1 JOHN 5:9–13; JOHN 17:6–19

Opening prayer

As this day welcomes us
with its challenges and joys,
we remember you are with us
every step along our way.
We commit this time to you,
a time of reflection,
a time of fellowship,
a time of worship,
a time to share the blessings
of your presence with us now.

Adoration

Blessed are those
whose delight is in you,
who are attentive
to the gentle whisper
of your call.
Blessed are those
who can set aside
the sound of this world
and meditate
on your word alone.

Like a fragrant blossom
from which a sweet perfume
diffuses in the summer breeze,
their prayerfulness
is a pleasant offering,
from which your Spirit
will bring fruitfulness
and glory to your name.

Confession

Forgiving God,
we bring to you our
incompleteness,
and ask that you
will make us whole.

We say the words
and sing the hymns,
but some days
we seem firmly anchored
in this kingdom
and not yours,
struggling
to find the faith
to carry on.

Forgiving God,
we bring to you our
incompleteness,
and ask that you
will make us whole.

Thanksgiving

We are an Easter people,
living your
resurrection life,
a mystery of faith
this world
cannot understand.
Receive our grateful thanks.

We are a chosen people,
accepting
your promise and word
inscribed upon our hearts,
our hope
of eternal life.
Receive our grateful thanks.

We are a praying people,
for the world
in which we are placed,
for neighbours and strangers,
all those
in need of your grace.
Receive our grateful thanks.

Day of Pentecost

ACTS 2:1–21; PSALM 104:24–34, 35B; ROMANS 8:22–27; JOHN 15:26–27; 16:4B–15

Opening prayer

Loving Father,
be the focus of our lives
as we meet together in your
  name.

Precious Jesus,
be the cornerstone on which,
step by step, our faith is built.

Holy Spirit,
be the flame that never dims
or gets extinguished in these
  hearts.

Adoration

The Spirit came
and your church was born,
in wind and fire
and words of power.

The Spirit came,
blowing fear aside,
and in its place
made weak hearts stronger.

The Spirit came
as your word foretold,
with prophecy,
visions and wonder.

The Spirit came
and is here today,
to feed the hearts
of those that hunger.

Confession

We ask for your forgiveness
when we forget
the power that lies within
and trust instead
in human strength.

Remind us of Pentecost,
when so clearly
you transformed fearful souls,
by your Spirit, into
people of power.

Renew these hearts,
grown cold,
with flames of fire
as on that Pentecost,
that we might be
the church that you desire.

Thanksgiving

Thank you for a gift
that enables our prayer,
reads our hearts
and guides us on our journey.

Thank you for a gift
that empowers the church
and gives it strength
to speak your word boldly.

Thank you for a gift
that builds up your body
and makes it
a blessing for others.

Thank you for the gift
of your Holy Spirit,
your presence in
these hearts and this world.

Trinity Sunday

ISAIAH 6:1–8; PSALM 29; ROMANS 8:12–17; JOHN 3:1–17

Opening prayer

As we join in worship today,
let us spend a moment in
quietness.

Listen to the noises coming
from outside this building—
people talking, vehicles going
by and maybe an aeroplane
passing overhead.

These are the sounds of
individuals who, mostly, have
chosen a different path for
their lives. They too need to
know the love and grace of
God, and may only gain this
knowledge if people like us
show it to them, through the
words we say and the lives we
live. *(Silence)*

Lord, as we draw near in
  worship,
we ask for your blessing
not only on this time together,
but also on our lives,
that by your Spirit
we might bring glory to you
and draw others
to your throne of grace.

Adoration

How can we respond
to God's glory
reflected in rainbow's arc,
starry night or eagle's flight?
How can we respond
to God's mercy
reflected in outstretched arms,
cruel nails and crown of
  thorns?

How can we respond
but to join the chorus of heaven
in their glorious song of praise:

'Holy, holy, holy
is the Lord Almighty;
the whole earth
is full of his glory!'

Confession

Your Spirit brings freedom,
but so often our lives
are weighed down
by burdens we carry within us.
Forgive us, Lord, we pray.

Your Spirit brings peace,
but so often our lives
are ill at ease,
concerned with what the day
  will bring us.
Forgive us, Lord, we pray.

Your Spirit brings wisdom,
yet we find it so hard
to recognise
your gentle whisper speaking
  to us.
Forgive us, Lord, we pray.

May we know the power
that breaks these chains that
  bind
our hearts and souls,
and grace to live the life
  you give.
Renew us, Lord, we pray.

Thanksgiving

Thank you for the good news
that the creator and lover
of the universe
took on flesh and bone
and stepped upon the earth,
rubbed shoulders with
people like us
and showed how far
love is prepared to go.

Thank you for the good news
that Jesus Christ died
and rose to life
so that people like us,
God's prodigals,
might turn around
and, seeing those outstretched
  arms,
be welcomed home.

Proper 4

Sunday between 29 May and 4 June (if after Trinity Sunday)

1 SAMUEL 3:1–10 [11–20]; PSALM 139:1–6, 13–18; 2 CORINTHIANS 4:5–12;
MARK 2:23—3:6

Opening prayer

In the quiet of this moment
we seek your presence, Lord—
the sure knowledge
that you are with us…
 (pause)
your gentle whisper speaking…
 (pause)
your Holy Spirit guiding…
 (pause)
your precious love abiding…
 (pause)

In the quiet of this moment
we seek your presence, Lord.

Adoration

We can put our trust in you,
 Lord,
because you know us so well;
you understand our thoughts
 and ways,
read the prayers upon our
 hearts,
are there beside us as we fall
and love us just as we are.

Leader: God of grace
All: Be close to us, we pray.

We can put our trust in you,
 Lord,
because you know the path we
 tread,
having walked this way before,
and, despite the weakness of
 our faith
and temptations we daily face,
you love us just as we are.

Leader: God of grace
All: Be close to us, we pray.

Confession

Forgive us, who call you
  'Lord',
pray to you,
yet do not hear your answer
as we're too engrossed
  elsewhere.
When you speak to us, Lord,
in the quiet of mountaintop
or bustle of a city street,
in our conversations
and deliberations,
at boardroom table
or kitchen sink,
may our response be always
that of a faithful Samuel:
'Speak, Lord, for your servant
is listening to your call.'

Thanksgiving

For all your saints who,
through centuries past,
have laid down their lives
for the sake of Jesus Christ,
we offer our grateful thanks.
(Pause)

For all who suffer today
for the sake of their faith,
and refuse to renounce
the name of Jesus Christ,
we offer our grateful thanks.
(Pause)

For all of those gathered here
who have responded in faith
when seeing in others
the light of Jesus Christ,
we offer our grateful thanks.

Year B

Proper 5

Sunday between 5 and 11 June (if after Trinity Sunday)

1 SAMUEL 8:4–11 [12–15] 16–20 [11:14–15]; PSALM 138; 2 CORINTHIANS 4:13—5:1;
MARK 3:20–35

Opening prayer

Throughout the world
your children meet,
in cities, towns,
villages,
refugee camps,
wherever they are able.
So we add our voice to theirs
in a symphony of praise
with the heavenly chorus.

Adoration

Your word is trustworthy;
generation after generation
has seen your truth
break through this world
into hearts and souls,
where it can
grow,
  blossom
and glorify your name.

Your love is everlasting;
generation after generation
has been blessed
by putting faith in you,
walking in your footsteps
and living lives
that simply,
  humbly,
glorify your name.

Confession

Forgive us, Lord,
when our lives are so busy
that our eyes are diverted
by the temporary pleasures
of this world
  and away
    from eternity.

Forgive us, Lord,
when momentary troubles
occupy our daylight hours
and the burden is too heavy
to carry,
  yet we fail
    to kneel at your feet.

Keep our eyes on you, Lord,
our strength and refuge,
for on your mercy
we can trust and depend.

Thanksgiving

For love
that values even us—
so undeserving,
so prone to failing,
so hesitant in our faith—
we offer our grateful thanks.

For love
that blesses and guides us
who often wander,
whose faith is tender,
who constantly need your help,
we offer our grateful thanks.

For love,
without which
we would be nothing
and, when possessing,
are everything,
we offer our grateful thanks.

Year B

Proper 6

Sunday between 12 and 18 June (if after Trinity Sunday)

1 SAMUEL 15:34—16:13; PSALM 20; 2 CORINTHIANS 5:6–10 [11–13] 14–17;
MARK 4:26–34

Opening prayer

We are gathered in worship.
Let us put aside the worries of
  this day
and focus on the reason that
  brings us to this place:

*(Pause for a moment after each
phrase)*

To be in the presence of our
  Lord and Saviour...
To bring our hymns and songs
  of praise...
To share in prayer the concerns
  of our heart...
To listen to God's word for our
  lives...
To enjoy the sweet blessings of
  fellowship...
To go out into the world
  refreshed for service...

Lord, bless this time together,
  we pray,
and be the blessing that we
  take with us
wherever we might go.

Adoration

Lord, you do not consider,
as we might,
the outward appearance
of anyone
in the granting of your blessing
and grace.
You look beyond outward show
to the heart,
seeing potential that lies
deep within,
that can be transformed by
your Spirit
into gifts that will bring glory
to your name.
Lord, you have welcomed us
as your own
and will, in your good time,
equip us for service.

Confession

When our hearts are not in the
 right place,
our lives are a struggle
and there's fragility in our faith,
we are drawn to you in humility,
asking for forgiveness.

Leader: God of mercy and grace
All: Forgive us.

When our lives do not reflect
the light that we remember
from the time we first believed,
we are drawn to the source of all
 we are,
asking for forgiveness.

Leader: God of mercy and grace
All: Forgive us.

When the seed that has been sown
does not flourish
and faith has yet to blossom,
we are drawn to the one who
 brings us life,
asking for forgiveness.

Leader: God of mercy and grace
All: Forgive us.

Thanksgiving

For all who are sowers
in this, your garden,
who scatter kindness,
beauty,
truth and love
into the rich earth
which you have prepared,
we give thanks.

We pray that seed thus sown
might be fed and watered
by your Spirit,
germinate,
grow
and produce a harvest
that is pleasing in your sight,
fit for a banquet
in your kingdom.

Proper 7

Sunday between 19 and 25 June (if after Trinity Sunday)

1 SAMUEL 17:[1A, 4–11, 19–23] 32–49; PSALM 9:9–20; 2 CORINTHIANS 6:1–13;
MARK 4:35–41

Opening prayer

We come into your presence,
Father, Son and Spirit,
Holy Trinity.

We come to worship
the one who made us,
the one who saves us,
the one who sustains us.

Holy Trinity,
Father, Son and Spirit,
we come into your presence.

Adoration

For those who seek you, Lord,
you are a safe refuge,
a stronghold
when circumstances
conspire against us
and we have nowhere else
   to turn.

For those who seek you, Lord,
you are the word of truth,
your Spirit
giving wisdom
when faith is tested,
so we can bear witness to
   your name.

For those who seek you, Lord,
you are the source of life,
for your love,
like living water,
pours into our hearts
and brings us to your feet
   in praise.

Confession

If anything we say or do
should cause one
of your dear ones
to stumble,
please, Lord, forgive us.
Sometimes we fail to see
the potential damage
our words and actions
can cause.

Grant us wisdom
and understanding
in all our relationships,
and remind us,
before we act or speak,
that we are building blocks
in your kingdom,
and stones can hurt others.

Thanksgiving

It's good to know
in stormy days
that wind and waves
obey your word,
and in the midst
of our distress
your calming voice
can still be heard.

Proper 8

Sunday between 26 June and 2 July

2 SAMUEL 1:1, 17–27; PSALM 130; 2 CORINTHIANS 8:7–15; MARK 5:21–43

Opening prayer

God of creation
and creativity,
be the inspiration
in our worship today.
May it not be stale
with familiarity,
but alive with
your spontaneity.
God of creation
and creativity,
be the inspiration
in our worship today.

Adoration

Ever-present God,
you walk with us
through good times
and bad,
on mountaintop
and valley floor;
your footsteps our guide,
your hands our support.

Ever-present God,
you are with us
when life is smooth
or rough,
in wholeness
and brokenness;
your healing our hope,
your touch our desire.

We shall fear nothing
if you are with us,
our ever-present God.

Confession

Healing God,
we come to you
seeking wholeness
for body and mind,
yet we so often fail
to understand
what we are asking for.
There is more to healing
than lack of pain,
more to wholeness
than lack of fear.

Help us bring to you
not just our hurting
but the pain we cause,
not just our brokenness
but the stones we throw,
not just our disease
but our dis-ease.

Healing God,
take our brokenness,
all that causes you pain,
and make us whole.

Thanksgiving

In you alone can we
have confidence;
in you alone can we
place our trust,
for in you alone is
forgiveness
and redemption
from all that we have done
and not done.
In you alone is
anointing,
empowerment
for all that we've become.

In you alone can we
have confidence,
for we have journeyed far
with you, Lord,
and shall continue,
until in fullness of time
we see you face to face.

We give you thanks for your
unfailing love
and faithfulness.

Proper 9

Sunday between 3 and 9 July

2 SAMUEL 5:1–5, 9–10; PSALM 48; 2 CORINTHIANS 12:2–10; MARK 6:1–13

Opening prayer

Speak to us, Lord,
through your word,
the hymns we shall sing
and the prayers
in our hearts.
Be the blessing
that we find as we gather here,
and the message
that we share,
to the glory of your name.

Adoration

Leader: Great is our God
All: And worthy of our praise.

This universe
and everything within it,
crafted with passion,
gifted in love.

Leader: Great is our God
All: And worthy of our praise.

This people,
created for a purpose,
to love and be loved,
made for service.

Leader: Great is our God
All: And worthy of our praise.

This fellowship
and all who belong to it,
blessed beyond measure,
called to worship.

Leader: Great is our God
All: And worthy of our praise.

Confession

We come to you
in our weakness
and brokenness,
aware that our lives
fall short of perfection,
at times bringing
a tear to your eye.
We come in humility,
asking for mercy
and forgiveness.

Remind us,
as we are tempted
in our daily walk,
that your grace
is all that we require,
and even in our weakness
your strength can be discerned.

Thanksgiving

Gracious Lord,
your love is greater
than any words can express,
pouring into hearts
left open to receive,
bringing healing
and restoration
where there is brokenness,
and peace of mind
where there is fear or stress.
You often use these vessels,
fragile though we are,
as the means by which
your blessing flows.

For such love,
undeserved
but gratefully received
and shared,
we offer grateful thanks.

Proper 10

Sunday between 10 and 16 July

2 SAMUEL 6:1–5, 12B–19; PSALM 24; EPHESIANS 1:3–14; MARK 6:14–29

Opening prayer

Creator God,
you have blessed us
in the dawning of this new day,
whether by sun's warm rays
or soft rainfall.
Accept, we pray,
this our offering of praise
for your gracious provision
and steadfast love.

Adoration

On our journey of faith,
you are with us as we walk,
encouraging, teaching,
lifting us when we stumble,
guiding us along the road.
And on mountaintop,
resting for a while,
you draw nearer still
and sit with us in quietness.

For such experiences
we bring our praise,
and ask that on our journey
you might lead us
not only in green pastures
but to higher ground as well,
where we might rest with you
and be refreshed.

Confession

Lord God, in your presence
we are aware of our sin,
our pride,
　selfishness,
　　lack of humility,
the desire to go our way,
　not yours.

You have lavished on us
the riches of your grace
and we have squandered
this precious gift
for temporary gain.

Forgive and renew our faith,
that our lives might bring
glory to your name
not tears to your eyes.

Thanksgiving

Thank you, Lord,
for reminding us,
as we stand politely
singing hymns and
reciting liturgy,
that your servant David,
when so moved,
raised his voice,
lifted his hands
and danced before you,
leapt and danced before you,
worshipped with
body,
　soul
　　and spirit.

Free us, Lord,
　just a little,
to express more openly
the gratitude in our hearts.

Year B

Proper 11

Sunday between 17 and 23 July

2 SAMUEL 7:1–14A; PSALM 89:20–37; EPHESIANS 2:11–22; MARK 6:30–34, 53–56

Opening prayer

In the presence of Father,
Son and Holy Spirit,
three in one,
we offer this
our sacrifice
of worship and praise.

In the presence of each other,
in openness and truth
we affirm
our unity
as family,
one body in Christ.

Adoration

We who were once far off—
who wandered as if
in a wilderness
searching for water,
desperate for shade—
now rest in your embrace,
feast on your word,
drink from a well
that will never run dry,
and have found the place
we were searching for,
as Christ has brought us home.

Confession

When we forget
that we are forgiven
of all that causes darkness in
  our lives,
remind us of the grace and
  peace
that brought us to this place.

When we forget
that we are your children
and your name is on our
  hearts,
remind us of the Son of God
who brought us to this place.

When we forget
that we have been chosen
and equipped to do your work,
remind us of the power of love
that brought us to this place.

Thanksgiving

For eternal love,
which has no boundaries
of time or season.

Leader: Loving Father
All: Accept our grateful thanks.

For patient love,
which is more enduring
than gold or silver.

Leader: Loving Father
All: Accept our grateful thanks.

For gracious love,
which is so forgiving
and freely given.

Leader: Loving Father
All: Accept our grateful thanks.

For the gift of love,
which is ours for sharing
with friend or stranger.

Leader: Loving Father
All: Accept our grateful thanks.

Proper 12

Sunday between 24 and 30 July

2 SAMUEL 11:1–15; PSALM 14; EPHESIANS 3:14–21; JOHN 6:1–21

Opening prayer

In this time of gathering
and as we make our way
  home,
be a constant presence—
a hand to hold,
  a voice to hear.
Make your dwelling in these
  hearts
and reveal to us the height
  and depth
of the love that brought us
  here to worship,
that your name might be
  glorified
here and in these lives.

Adoration

You, whose love
is deeper than oceans;
whose love
is higher than mountains;
whose love
dwells in the heart and soul
of lives deeply rooted in you;
heavenly Father,
it is you we serve,
you alone we worship
and to you alone all glory is
  due.

The fool says in his heart,
'There is no God.'
As for us, we shall proclaim,
'Our God reigns!'

Confession

Forgive us, Lord,
when we fail to share
the love that has been given,
when the basket
of loaves and fishes
we have feasted upon
is not passed on,
that others might be fed.
Forgive our selfishness
and the damage done.

May ours be willing hands,
voices quick to share
the truth we know;
may our lives bring a blessing
to those whose hearts touch
 ours.

Thanksgiving

From your riches
you have poured
such blessings
into our hearts,
opened our eyes
to the height, width
and depth of your love,
strengthened our faith,
empowered our lives,
gifted us for service
through your Holy Spirit,
and enabled us
to walk with confidence
the path prepared for us.

The fool might say
there is no God,
but we were blind
and now we see.
Hallelujah!

Proper 13

Sunday between 31 July and 6 August

2 SAMUEL 11:26—12:13A; PSALM 51:1–12; EPHESIANS 4:1–16; JOHN 6:24–35

Opening prayer

Into your presence
we come as children
within the loving family
of our heavenly Father.
Bless this time together
and our sacrifice of praise,
that your name alone
might be glorified in this place.

Adoration

Risen Saviour,
by your Spirit
you breathe life into this
   world;
feed your children,
sustain the weak.

Those who seek you
do not go hungry;
they are fed by the word of
   life.
Those who believe in you
will never thirst;
they are refreshed by living
   water.

Risen Saviour,
by your Spirit
you breathe life into this world
and fill our souls with praise.

Confession

When our hearts condemn us
for careless words,
selfish thoughts
or actions we know might
  hurt:

Leader: Create in us a pure
  heart, O God
**All: And renew a right spirit
  within us.**

When our souls are burdened
and once again
we're tempted
by the wisdom of this world:

Leader: Create in us a pure
  heart, O God
**All: And renew a right spirit
  within us.**

When your word reminds us
that our sin affects
even you,
bringing tears to your eyes:

Leader: Create in us a pure
  heart, O God
**All: And renew a right spirit
  within us.**

Thanksgiving

God of mercy,
in you we find forgiveness,
acceptance in your presence
and the hope of new life.

God of humility,
in you we find perfect love;
you are the servant-king,
  the bread of life
whose blood was shed for us.

God of power,
in you we find the Spirit
who brings us healing,
  wholeness
and strength to face each day.

Receive our grateful thanks,
  O God,
for all your gifts to us.

Proper 14

Sunday between 7 and 13 August

2 SAMUEL 18:5–9, 15, 31–33; PSALM 130; EPHESIANS 4:25—5:2; JOHN 6:35, 41–51

Opening prayer

God of love,
you who hold this world
  within your loving hands,
be with us in our worship
  today.

God of peace,
you who walked this earth to
  bring your people home,
be with us in our worship
  today.

God of hope,
you who bring us life and live
  within our hearts,
be with us in our worship
  today.

Adoration

God of summer sun,
fruitful fields
and food to eat,
you are worthy of our praise.

God of mountain stream,
rolling hills
and pleasant views,
you are worthy of our praise.

God of truth and light,
bread of life
and saving grace,
you are worthy of our praise.

God of all we are,
three in one,
Lord of all,
you are worthy of our praise.

Confession

You have blessed us
in so many ways,
and in return
we have failed you
in so many ways.

You show forgiveness
and we harbour resentment.
You show compassion
and we turn away.
In so many ways
we fail to live
the life we profess.

As we confess,
help us once more
to follow your example,
living a life of love
as Jesus Christ loved us—
a pleasing sacrifice to you.

Thanksgiving

Bread of Life, you feed us
through word and sacrament,
that we might feed others,
the bread we share
a remembrance
of your presence with us.
Strengthen us for service,
that seeds we sow
might grow and flourish,
and words we share
might bring glory to your
  name.

Bread of Life, you feed us
through word and sacrament,
that we might feed others.

Thanks be to your name.

Proper 15

Sunday between 14 and 20 August

1 KINGS 2:10–12; 3:3–14; PSALM 111; EPHESIANS 5:15–20; JOHN 6:51–58

Opening prayer

We are here to bring
our offering of praise
to the one who made us
and the one who calls us.

We are here to bring
our offering of prayer
to the one who loves us
and the one who hears us.

We are here to bring
the offering of our lives
to the one who saves us
and brings us to this place.

Adoration

We will bring to you our praise
this and every day,
in sacred places
and working places,
in the songs we sing
and the whispers of our heart.
For you are gracious
and compassionate,
slow to anger,
rich in mercy,
abounding in love.
You have blessed us through
    our lives
and we will bring to you our
    praise
this and every day.

Confession

When our hearts are fixed
on earthly things
and our minds distracted
from the eternal,
remind us of Solomon
who, when asked what he
  desired,
did not choose earthly wealth
or place of honour,
but wisdom
to discern right from wrong.

Forgive us, Lord,
when we misuse the freedom
you have given us,
confusing the wisdom of this
  world
with the truth of your own.
Grant us discernment
to know the difference
and trust in you alone.

Thanksgiving

When the journey is long
and we hunger and thirst,
Bread of Life, you sustain us.

When the road is hard
and our bodies weak,
Bread of Life, you heal us.

When our spirits are low
and we can't carry on,
Bread of Life, you revive us.

When we offer our hands
in service and love,
Bread of Life, you bless us.

When the challenge is great
and the workers are few,
Bread of Life, you empower us.

When the victory is won
and we see your face,
Bread of Life, you will rejoice
  with us.

Thank you for feeding us
in so many ways.

Proper 16

Sunday between 21 and 27 August

1 KINGS 8:[1, 6, 10–11] 22–30, 41–43; PSALM 84; EPHESIANS 6:10–20; JOHN 6:56–69

Opening prayer

In our meeting together,
we bring to you all those
who would be here
but for their infirmity,
asking that they might know
the joy of your presence
wherever they might be,
and, joining with us in spirit
in this offering of worship,
be blessed as we are.

Adoration

We are blessed indeed,
who have put our trust in you,
who live to serve
and, in our walk of faith,
go where you might lead us.

We are blessed indeed,
who have found our strength
  in you,
who seek your face
and hear that quiet whisper
as you encourage us.

We are blessed indeed,
who bow down to worship
  you,
then go out
in faith to do the tasks
you have prepared for us.

Confession

Forgive us, Lord,
when we rely on our own
  strength
and not yours,
failing to make use
of the spiritual armour you
  provide,
and are wounded in the fight.

Forgive us, Lord,
when we forget your provision
and your love,
listening instead
to the insistent voices of this
  world,
and struggle to know what's
  right.

Draw us close, Lord;
equip us with all that we need;
empower us;
strengthen our faith
so we can engage with this
  present world
under the banner of your light.

Thanksgiving

In your word, O Lord,
we can put our trust;
to you we can turn
when struggling to cope,
when faith is confused
and it's wisdom we seek.

In your word, O Lord,
we can put our trust;
to you we can turn
when the world closes in,
sin drags us down
and we're back at your feet.

In your word
we find wholeness and peace,
enough for each day.
In your word
we find hope for tomorrow,
such mercy and grace.
In your word, O Lord,
we can put our trust
completely.

Proper 17

Sunday between 28 August and 3 September

SONG OF SOLOMON 2:8–13; PSALM 45:1–2, 6–9; JAMES 1:17–27;
MARK 7:1–8, 14–15, 21–23

Opening prayer

Into your presence,
Lord, we come,
bringing our offering of praise
and the service of our lives
wherever you might lead us
within this, your beautiful
but needy world.

Adoration

All we are,
all we have
and all that we can be
is laid at your feet, Lord.
(Pause)

May our lives,
rooted in love,
be your hands and voice,
bringing healing and grace.
(Pause)

May the world,
looking at us,
see instead a light
that has its source in you.
(Pause)

May the truth
sown in our hearts
bear fruit in our lives
and bring glory to you.
(Pause)

All we are,
all we have
and all that we can be
is laid at your feet, Lord.

Confession

You call us to be your hands
  and voice
and walk the path you trod,
to bring your love to those we
  meet,
to show compassion,
fight injustice,
help the weak.
You call us to be not just
  hearers
but doers of your word,
to be the face of Christ that
  others see.

When we fail you,
which is often,
please forgive, we pray.
You call us to be your hands
  and voice;
grant us the faith to become
the people you would have
  us be—
agents of change in this,
your world.

Thanksgiving

We give thanks for all
whose lives reflect the life
  of Christ,
whose words bring wisdom,
compassion, peace;
whose hands bring healing,
support, relief;
whose feet will walk the
  extra mile
if there should be a need,
and, in obedience to their
  Lord,
share a word or two of grace.

We give thanks for all
whose lives reflect that
  of Christ,
and pray that we
might also live that life.

Year B

Proper 18

Sunday between 4 and 10 September

PROVERBS 22:1–2, 8–9, 22–23; PSALM 125; JAMES 2:1–10 [11–13] 14–17; MARK 7:24–37

Opening prayer

Bless us, Lord,
in this time together.
Be in our worship,
the prayers that are on our
  hearts
and the burdens we bear.
Be in our conversations,
the sharing of joys and
  sorrows,
and the service of our lives.
In this time together,
bless us, Lord, we pray.

Adoration

Our faith is built
on a sure foundation
of eternal love and grace,
stones that cannot be broken.

Our faith is built
into a holy temple
where God's Spirit moves
  freely
and beauty and joy reside.

Our faith is built
by a master builder
to withstand the mightiest
  storm
and keep safe all those inside.

Our faith is built
by God our maker.

Confession

Gracious Father, in our walk
 with you
we often find ourselves
on difficult terrain,
in need of your steadying hand
to keep us on our feet
and guide us on your way
 once more.
Forgive the unsteadiness of
 our faith,
as we wander from your word,
distracted by the world
and stumbling into sin.
Raise us to greater things,
enlarge our vision,
and bring us to a grateful
and complete obedience to
 you.

Thanksgiving

God of compassion,
whose love brings healing
to lives that are broken
and, to the hungry, bread;
whose word is comfort
to those walking in darkness
and grace to those in need,
we bring you our grateful
 thanks.

God of compassion,
whose love has no end
and no beginning
yet lives within our hearts;
whose grace is precious,
beyond understanding
yet offered to us all,
we bring you our grateful
 thanks.

Year B

Proper 19

Sunday between 11 and 17 September

PROVERBS 1:20–33; PSALM 19; JAMES 3:1–12; MARK 8:27–38

Opening prayer

In your presence
we find the bread of life
that will feed our souls.

In your presence
we find living water
that will quench our thirst.

In your presence
we find the Lamb of God
who forgives our sin.

In your presence
we find radiance and light
in which to worship.

Adoration

The heavens declare your
  glory;
the skies proclaim your praise.
No words are spoken,
no sounds are heard,
yet within their majesty
your artistry is revealed.

Open our eyes and
  imaginations,
that we might see
within the ordinary
the hand of the divine,
and rejoice in this world
in which we live and move,
for it is your gift of love to us.

Confession

Forgive us when we fail to see
your hand within the beauty
  of this world,
or your love in the comforting
  words
of a friend or stranger.
Forgive us when we fail to
  hear
your whisper cut through the
  clutter of this world,
or to listen as you speak
  through quietness
into the depth of our hearts.

Open these eyes to see,
these ears to hear,
these minds to understand
and these lives to serve,
that the words we utter
and the thoughts within our
  hearts
might be pleasing in your sight,
our strength and our redeemer.

Thanksgiving

To some you are
comfortable words
in times of sorrow or need;
to others, a teacher
dying for what he believed.
To some you are
nothing more than
a purveyor of magic tricks.

But to us you are
this world's creator,
this world's saviour,
the breath of life
sustaining us each day,
to whom we raise
our hearts and souls
in ever grateful thanks.

Proper 20

Sunday between 18 and 24 September

PROVERBS 31:10–31; PSALM 1; JAMES 3:13—4:3, 7–8A; MARK 9:30–37

Opening prayer

Eternal God,
by whom this world was made,
to you belongs our praise.

Precious Jesus,
who died that we might live,
to you belongs our praise.

Holy Spirit,
who lives within our hearts,
to you belongs our praise.

Three in One,
who draw us here by grace,
to you belongs our praise.

Adoration

To whom shall we turn
  for wisdom,
when you are the source of
  everything wise?

To whom shall we turn
  for mercy,
when you are the source of the
  love that we seek?

To whom shall we turn
  for compassion and peace,
when hearts are low and our
  faith is so weak?

To the one who is
  the source
of everything we seek; to you,
  dear Lord, we turn.

Confession

Forgive us, Lord,
when the road we travel
is of our own choosing
and we are distracted
by the sights and sounds
that surround us.

Forgive us, Lord,
when your voice is muffled
by the noise of our lives
and we lose the path,
finding ourselves alone.

Be with us;
guard and guide us, we pray;
keep our eyes and ears
focused on you,
and bring us safely
through each day.

Thanksgiving

You cherish the humble
above the proud,
and bless those
who put others first,
taking their example
from that of their Lord.

You turn around
the values of this world
and invite us to
participate
in a way of living
where the first shall be last,
the last shall be first,
and the blessed in the kingdom
will be servants of all.

Thank you for the gift of
  courage, Lord,
to step out
and dare to be different.

Proper 21

Sunday between 25 September and 1 October

ESTHER 7:1–6, 9–10; 9:20–22; PSALM 124; JAMES 5:13–20; MARK 9:38–50

Opening prayer

In our gathering today,
we join the angels
in bringing our worship
and fellowship
as a sweet-smelling offering
to you, O Lord.

Adoration

To you we turn
in times of plenty,
when hearts are light
and filled with praise.

To you we turn
in times of sorrow,
when hearts are heavy
and filled with prayer.

To you we turn
in every season,
source of all blessing,
here in our meeting,
our comforter,
healer
and Lord.

Confession

Forgive us, Lord,
when our thoughts
are more concerned with self
than the needs of neighbour.
Bring to our minds
the image of our Saviour, who,
though carrying such a task,
found time for those in need,
offered healing to the sick
and showed compassion for
  the weak.

Give us a heart that reaches out
beyond these walls
to those who are passing by,
and enable us to become
the faithful disciples
you long for us to be.

Thanksgiving

Thank you, Lord,
for all those saints
who, by the way they live,
show they belong to you:
those working with
their hands or intellect;
those making difficult
decisions of state;
all whose diligent labour
and honest endeavour,
carried out with love,
affect the lives of others
and carry the imprint of you.

Thank you, Lord,
for all those saints
who, by the way they live,
show they belong to you.

Proper 22

Sunday between 2 and 8 October

JOB 1:1; 2:1–10; PSALM 26; HEBREWS 1:1–4; 2:5–12; MARK 10:2–16

Opening prayer

In your house
and in the presence of your
  people,
we declare that you are
the one who made us,
the one who loves us,
the one who saved us
and the one who brings us
  here to worship
in humble gratitude and praise.

Adoration

We worship you,
Father, Son and Spirit,
glorious Trinity,
through whom
stars were flung into space
and life was breathed
into this place that we call
  home;
through whom
prophets spoke out in faith
and spread the word of grace
that comes from you.

We worship you,
Father, Son and Spirit,
glorious mystery,
for in the light of the Son
we see the Father's face,
and in the words of the Son
we hear the Spirit's voice,
three in one,
first and last.

Confession

We will praise you
and we will serve you,
not only here
but wherever you send us,
in this, your neighbourhood;
in this, your world.
We will be your hands
reaching out to those in need;
your words
bringing comfort, setting
  others free.

Examine our hearts, therefore,
and if you find anything
that hinders our effectiveness,
take it away
and in its place
pour in your Spirit,
so that our lives might bring
a blessing to this world
and a smile upon your face.

Thanksgiving

Loving God, thank you that
  you do not question
the theological and political
  views
or denominational differences
of those who bow before your
  throne;
you do not look for a particular
  virtue
or provide disclaimer forms
before you hear our prayers.

All you ask is to see within
  our eyes
the simple faith of a child,
an openness to follow
and a willingness to grow into
the people you would have us
  become,
in the fellowship of your
  kingdom,
wherever we might be.

Proper 23

Sunday between 9 and 15 October

JOB 23:1–9, 16–17; PSALM 22:1–15; HEBREWS 4:12–16; MARK 10:17–31

Opening prayer

Living God,
we come into your
  presence
to feed upon your word,
to listen to your voice
and know your risen power
in this place
and in our lives.

Adoration

To whom shall we lift our praises
except to you, Creator God,
who fashioned this world
from the fabric of space
and filled it with such beauty
for us to enjoy.

Leader: Lord, your name is exalted
All: And we shall sing your praises.

To whom shall we lift our praises
except to you, Eternal God.
From the dawn of time
we were part of your plan
and to the end of time
we are held in your hand.

Leader: Lord, your name is exalted
All: And we shall sing your praises.

To whom shall we lift our praises
except to you, Almighty God,
who grants us freedom
from the burden of sin
and, as shepherd, brings us
safely home again.

Leader: Lord, your name is exalted
All: And we shall sing your praises.

Confession

Forgive us, Lord,
when our faith is too small
to believe you can help us;
when we cry in the dark
not expecting an answer.

Forgive us, Lord,
when the wise of the world
try so hard to persuade us
that you do not exist,
and we're tempted to listen.

Forgive us, Lord,
when the journey of faith
is a hard path to follow
and no longer the joy
it was when we first began.

Forgive us, Lord;
rekindle the flame
that once shone
within these hearts, we pray.

Thanksgiving

In you, O God,
is our waking
and our resting.

In you, O God,
is our healing
and forgiving.

In you, O God,
is our praying
and receiving.

In you, O God,
is our giving
and our blessing.

Receive our thanks
and praise.

Proper 24

Sunday between 16 and 22 October

JOB 38:1–7 [34–41]; PSALM 104:1–9, 24, 35C; HEBREWS 5:1–10; MARK 10:35–45

Opening prayer

Creator God,
reveal yourself to us
through your eternal word.

Precious Jesus,
reveal yourself through us
in the love that we share.

Holy Spirit,
reveal yourself in us
through the gifts that we use.

Three in One,
be the life within us
as we journey with you.

Adoration

For your word,
active as a sharpened sword,
cutting through the wisdom of
   this world,
we praise you.

For your word,
a light into the darkness,
reaching to the heart of who
   we are,
we praise you.

For your word,
revealing your majesty,
drawing us into your loving
   arms,
we praise you.

Confession

Forgive us, Lord, when our
  prayers
are all about self
and our focus is simply
on what we expect to receive.

Remind us of all you have
  done for us,
that we might sing your
  praises.
Remind us of all that you
  mean to us,
that we might share your story.
Remind us of all that you ask
  of us,
that we might turn to service.

Forgive us, Lord, when our
  prayers
are all about self;
may our focus be simply
upon you, our neighbour
and this, your beautiful world.

Thanksgiving

Thank you, O Lord,
for the earth on which we
  walk,
each mountaintop,
the sunlit sky.

Thank you, O Lord,
for the beauty that we see,
fragrant flower,
butterfly.

Thank you, O Lord,
for the peace within our hearts
when filled with joy
or sorrow.

Thank you, O Lord,
for the journey that we make,
your footsteps that
we follow.

Proper 25

Sunday between 23 and 29 October

JOB 42:1–6, 10–17; PSALM 34:1–8 [19–22]; HEBREWS 7:23–28; MARK 10:46–52

Opening prayer

It is good to be here
in this, your house, Lord,
meeting with family,
sharing fellowship,
bringing our offering
of service and praise.
It is good to be here
in this, your house, Lord.

Adoration

Oh, that others might know
  your name
and declare it in their lives,
that they might find the rock
from which our faith is hewn.

Oh, that others might know
  your love
and the freedom that it brings,
might journey to the cross
and find their hope in you.

Oh, that others might know
  the touch
of your Spirit on their lives,
and find the source from
  which
this living water flows.

Oh, that others might know
  you
as we do
in our hearts and lives,
and find wholeness, healing an
  peace.

Confession

When the way we live
does not reflect the God we
  serve,
forgive us.

When the love we give
expects something back in
  return,
forgive us.

When the words we speak
cause somebody else to
  stumble,
forgive us.

Have mercy; rekindle
this spark of faith
and by your Spirit
empower us.

Thanksgiving

Gracious Lord,
in you we find forgiveness
for our sin,
should we but ask.
In you we find the healing
that we seek,
should we but ask.

In you we find the reasons
to believe,
should we but ask.
In you we find the one who
sets us free,
should we but ask.

Gracious Lord,
you stand at the door
to our heart,
  and knock,
    and wait
to be invited in.

Thank you that you answer
if we will simply ask.

Year B

Fourth Sunday before Advent

Sunday between 30 October and 5 November

RUTH 1:1–18; PSALM 146; HEBREWS 9:11–14; MARK 12:28–34

Opening prayer

Together with your
  children,
wherever they might be,
we bring you our offering
  of praise,
the burdens on our hearts
and, as we feed on your
  word,
the service of our lives
as change-makers
in your beautiful
but fragile world.

Adoration

Leader: We are blessed indeed
All: Who put our trust in God.

We will praise you, Lord,
not only with our lips
but in our daily lives.
For you have called us your
  children
and welcomed us home.

Leader: We are blessed indeed
All: Who put our trust in God.

We will praise you, Lord,
for all that you have done
and promised through your Son.
For through the cross you have
  granted
forgiveness of sins.

Leader: We are blessed indeed
All: Who put our trust in God.

We will praise you, Lord, the one
who brings wholeness and peace,
lifts the weak and heals the sick.
For you are maker, creator
and source of our life.

Leader: We are blessed indeed
All: Who put our trust in God.

Confession

You call us to love
both you and neighbour
with heart and soul
and everything we are.
But we fail to heed this call;
we draw back from those in
  need
and choose this life we lead,
which is more interested in
  self.

Forgive us, you whose love
is the greatest gift of all,
whose grace extends beyond
  all that we can know.
Forgive us, and enable us
to be the people we could be.

Bless us, that we in turn
might become a blessing,
and your name
be on our lips each day.

Thanksgiving

It is a truth worth sharing,
  Lord,
that there is nothing
we can say or do
that will make you love us
  more,
and nothing we can say or do
that will make you love us less,
for in your eyes
we are all your children,
equally precious in your sight.

Such love, so undeserved,
poured out and overflowing,
so unlike the love
that we so often show,
demands a response,
not only in our prayer
but in the thanksgiving
  offering
of our daily lives.

All Saints Day

1 November or the first Sunday in November

WISDOM OF SOLOMON 3:1–9; ISAIAH 25:6–9; PSALM 24; REVELATION 21:1–6A;
JOHN 11:32–44

Opening prayer

We join the praise
of your saints from every age
in their heavenly chorus,
praying that, with them,
we might be counted
among your faithful people
in this place
and in our daily walk
with you.

Adoration

Who are your saints, Lord,
but those who do your will,
have clean hands
and a pure heart,
take up their cross
and follow where you lead?

Who are your saints, Lord,
but those who live to serve,
share your love
and grace,
meet together
and worship at your feet?

Who are your saints, Lord,
but those whom you have
  blessed
in this life,
who live
that they might share
eternity with you?

Confession

There are times, Lord,
when we feel like anything
but your saints,
and our thoughts,
words and actions
don't bring honour to your
  name.

There are times, Lord,
when our faith struggles
to survive,
and our minds
start to wonder
if we're travelling alone.

Forgive those times, Lord,
when we're stumbling
on the road,
and, by your grace,
ignite that spark
of faith to draw us back to you.

Thanksgiving

Your word promises
a new heaven
and a new earth,
where you will once again
walk within your garden,
as at Eden.

Your word promises
no more tears
and no more pain,
as the old passes away
and welcomes in the new
with you as king.

For the promise in your word
and the revelation
of that which is to come
for your children
who walk this earth,
we give our grateful thanks.

Third Sunday before Advent

Sunday between 6 and 12 November

RUTH 3:1–5; 4:13–17; PSALM 127; HEBREWS 9:24–28; MARK 12:38–44

Opening prayer

As we gather for worship,
let us remember
we are not an isolated
 community
of believers in this place,
but the family of God
gathered together
from every corner of this world
in one great offering of praise.

Adoration

Heavenly Father,
we love you,
worship and adore you,
and in humble service
kneel before you now.

Precious Jesus,
we love you,
worship and adore you,
and in obedience
listen for your call.

Holy Spirit,
we love you,
worship and adore you,
and put our trust securely
in your strength alone.

Three in One,
we love you,
worship and adore you.
Unite us in your grace
and your loving care.

Confession

We build the life
that we inhabit
on shallow ground,
with little skill,
no solid plan,
using stones that lie around,
and wonder,
in the storm,
why our efforts are in vain.

But unless you build this
  house,
how can it stand?
Unless you watch over us,
how can we feel secure?

Forgive us, Lord,
those times when we forget
in whom we need
to put our trust—
the master builder—
and bring us back to you.

Thanksgiving

Leader: You call to us, Lord
All: And we shall follow.

Lord, we thank you
that from the stony paths
on which we walk,
and the bruises of our
  stumbling,
you call us on to solid ground
where we can build a faith
that stands against the storms
  of life
and offers us protection.

Leader: You call to us, Lord
All: And we shall follow.

Lord, we thank you
that we can set aside
all that holds us back
and start again by following
when you call,
knowing that we walk
where you have been before,
a path that leads through death
  to life
in glorious resurrection.

Leader: You call to us, Lord
All: And we shall follow.

Second Sunday before Advent

Sunday between 13 and 19 November

PSALM 16; HEBREWS 10:11–14, (15–18), 19–25; MARK 13:1–8

Opening prayer

God the Father,
be the light that shines
  upon us.

God the Son,
be the love that dwells
  between us.

God the Spirit,
be the life that grows
  within us.

Three in One,
be the unity embracing us
this day and all days.

Adoration

God of grace and mercy,
we worship you alone.
In you is our trust,
our light for the path.
In you is our strength
when the going is tough.
In you is our peace
in sorrow or joy.
In you is our hope
of eternal life.
We worship you alone,
God of grace and mercy.

Confession

When your footsteps
seem unclear to us
and, on our journey,
our eyes are drawn
to a different
and seemingly
attractive path,
forgive us, who are
so easily distracted.
Forgive us, who lose
our sense of direction.
Forgive us, who stumble
and, falling, call to you.
Place our feet again
on the road
you have prepared for us
and bring us
safely home to you.

Thanksgiving

For a cross of wood
that was the cost
of this world's sin,
  we thank you.

For a crown of thorns
that showed the world
what kind of king you are,
  we thank you.

For a curtain torn
and, at your throne,
a welcoming,
  we thank you.

Christ the King

Sunday between 20 and 26 November

2 SAMUEL 23:1–7; PSALM 132:1–12 [13–18]; REVELATION 1:4B–8; JOHN 18:33–37

Opening prayer

May Christ our King
reign over us,
his love inspire us,
his footsteps guide us,
his peace be with us.
May Christ our King
reign over us,
now and always.

Adoration

Alpha and Omega,
first and last,
God before all beginnings,
who is and was
and is to come;
Almighty,
to whom all creatures
owe their existence,
to whom all angels sing,
by whom we receive
our full salvation;
we bring this offering,
for you are worthy of our
    praise.

Confession

Forgive us, Jesus,
when we struggle to explain
in simple and convincing
  words
who you are
and what you mean to us.

Forgive us when,
asked to defend our faith,
we hesitate
and seem to be unsure
of what we believe.

You know our hearts,
where your Spirit dwells;
grant us the confidence
to express in words
the love we have for you,
our Saviour and our King.

Thanksgiving

Thank you for grace shown
  to us,
undeserving as we are,
and may the grace that we
  receive
be reflected through our lives.

Thank you for peace sown
  within us,
calming our restless souls,
and may the peace that we
  receive
be reflected through our lives.

Thank you for love
  embracing us,
healing and warming hearts,
and may the love that we
  receive
be reflected through our lives.

May our lives become
an expression of your grace,
peace and love,
and a thanks offering
shared with those we meet.

Year C

First Sunday of Advent

Sunday between 27 November and 3 December

JEREMIAH 33:14–16; PSALM 25:1–9; 1 THESSALONIANS 3:9–13; LUKE 21:25–36

Opening prayer

This is Advent, a season of promise. In our worship we prepare for the birth of a baby in a dusty stable, and remind ourselves that this child will become the Saviour of the world, who will return again in power and glory to bring all of his children together in songs of everlasting praise.

The promise of the baby is also the promise of eternal life to all who believe.

God of hope and promise, be with us throughout this Advent season, and draw us ever closer as we travel together toward the stable and the birth of your Son, our Saviour Jesus Christ.

Adoration

God of majesty and promise, who spoke and this world was, who breathed and this world lived, who counts the hairs upon our heads, sees our thoughts, reads our hearts and loves us more than we deserve, how can we not bring to you this offering of praise?

For in the child at Bethlehem lies the promise of intimacy with a Saviour who would die even for me, and the promise of an eternity in which to praise you more each day. God of majesty and promise, we praise your holy name.

Confession

To you, O Lord, we bring our
  lives,
troubled, broken or at ease,
a sacrificial offering
for you to use.

Take away our selfishness
and teach us to love as you
  loved.
Take away our sense of pride
and show us the meaning of
  humility.
Take away our blindness
and show us the world
  through your eyes.
Take away our greed
and teach us how to give as
  you gave.

Show us your ways;
teach us your paths,
that we might walk with you
  more closely,
our hand in your hand,
our feet in your footprints,
eternal Lord who became
a baby in a stable.

Thanksgiving

For your word which endures,
we give you thanks.
For promises to hold,
we give you thanks.
For intimacy with you,
we give you thanks.
For the love that surrounds us,
we give you thanks.
For all those here today,
we give you thanks.
For family and friends,
we give you thanks.
For visitors among us,
we give you thanks.
For the hope of Advent time,
when we prepare to see
the divine step on to earth,
we give you thanks.

Year C

Second Sunday of Advent

Sunday between 4 and 10 December

BARUCH 5:1–9 OR MALACHI 3:1–4; LUKE 1:68–79; PHILIPPIANS 1:3–11; LUKE 3:1–6

Opening prayer

This is Advent, the season of preparation. The shops are full of gifts that we might give or receive. Streets are decorated, and choirs begin the rounds of community centres and retirement homes with their seasonal offerings of carols.

In our preparations we remember John the Baptist, who came to prepare the Jewish people for the arrival of Jesus—John, who would prepare a way through a call to repentance, so that hearts would be ready to receive the one who was to come.

Father God, prepare our hearts not only for the celebration to come but also for sharing that good news with friends, family and colleagues, should the opportunity arise. Grant us courage and a willingness to talk about the love that came down to earth and walked among us.

Adoration

As streets are thronged with shoppers,
bright lights and tempting offers,
Christmas songs and children's laughter,
you lead us along a different path
to a desert river and a prophetic voice.

A call to repentance.
A call to service.
A call to immerse ourselves
in living water that will never run dry.
A call to prepare a way in our own lives
for the Saviour of the world to enter in,
to know your touch of tender mercy
and rest in your forgiving love.

For your faithful prophets
and your living Word,
we bring this offering of praise.

Confession

You challenge us, this Advent
  time,
this season of anticipation,
to put aside our pride
and understand our need
for repentance,
forgiveness
and mercy.
Less of self, more of you.

You challenge us, this Advent
  time
in preparation for a pilgrimage
to the stable and beyond.
Purify our hearts and thoughts,
for we are in the presence
of angels and
the incarnate God.

Thanksgiving

Thank you, Father, for your
  patience
with a rebellious people,
loving you one moment,
forgetting you the next.
Thank you for your endless
  love,
which does not give up
but wants the best for us,
despite our faults.
Thank you for your promise,
to all who believe
and put their trust in you,
of everlasting life.

In this Advent season
may the Baptist's call
resound in hearts and minds,
drawing many to your living
  water
where they might find
  forgiveness
and knowledge of your grace.

Third Sunday of Advent

Sunday between 11 and 17 December

ZEPHANIAH 3:14–20; ISAIAH 12:2–6; PHILIPPIANS 4:4–7; LUKE 3:7–18

Opening prayer

This is Advent, the season
of expectation. In homes
throughout the land,
Christmas cards stand on
mantelpiece and windowsill.
Festive trees are adorned
with tinsel and baubles, and
children wonder what gifts will
lie beneath the tree this year.

Two thousand years ago,
a people waited expectantly
as they listened to a prophet
called John speaking of one
who was to come, and they
began to prepare themselves to
meet him.

Father God, your servant John
the Baptist came with a a call
for repentance and lives to be
transformed. Those who heard
were filled with expectation,
waiting for the Messiah, and
yet they failed to notice his
arrival. This Advent, may we
too be filled with expectation
as we celebrate the greatest gift
of all—your Son, Jesus Christ.

Adoration

Rejoice in the Lord always!
Shout out his name,
for God is with us;
our God is with us,
the God of our salvation
in whom alone we trust.

Rejoice in the Lord always!
Shout out his name,
for God is our Father
who brings us home
by streams of living water
where we shall thirst no more.

Rejoice in the Lord always!
Shout out his name,
for he guides our way,
enabling us
to become the people
we were always made to be.

Rejoice in the Lord always!
Shout out his name,
for God is with us;
our God is with us.

Confession

Forgive us, Lord;
we are a wandering people
who kneel before you now,
bringing our prayers
and requests to your feet
when we have need of you,
then going our own way
when times are good
and life seems easy.

Forgive us;
teach us your paths,
that we might follow you
each and every day,
in sunshine and rain,
joy and sorrow,
enjoying your company
from the moment we awake
until we lay our heads to rest.

Thanksgiving

You are the Father
who welcomes home
the far-wandering prodigal.

You are the Father
who prepares a meal
while others walk away.

You are the Father
whose love extends
beyond our thoughts or minds.

You are the Father
who knows our hearts,
yet loves us as we are.

You are the Father
whose word we trust,
in whose arms we have no fear.

You are the Father
whose tender touch
makes a wounded spirit whole.

You are the Father
whose only Son
was born that he might die.

You are the Father
to whom we bring
our grateful thanks this day.

Fourth Sunday of Advent

Sunday between 18 and 24 December
MICAH 5:2–5A; LUKE 1:46–55; PSALM 80:1–7; HEBREWS 10:5–10; LUKE 1:39–45

Opening prayer

The preparations are in place,
the excitement mounts and,
for those who are travelling to
visit families, arrangements are
finalised, clothes sorted, gifts
wrapped and labelled.

Two thousand years ago
and more, a pregnant girl
called Mary visited her cousin
Elizabeth, who was also
expecting a child. As soon as
they greeted each other, the
baby in Elizabeth's womb
kicked out, and she saw this
as a sign that Mary was to be
greatly blessed by God.

Father God, when we consider
your servant Mary, we see
humility and obedience, so
often lacking in our own lives.
As we hear your word again
and consider the one through
whose body you entered
this world, remind us of the
meaning of humility and grant
us faith to know that your
promises are always fulfilled.

Adoration

My soul magnifies the Lord!
All is ready—
stable prepared,
shepherds working,
magi journeying,
gifts chosen.

My soul magnifies the Lord!
A city awaits,
crowded, bustling;
stars are shining,
people expecting,
a drama unfolding.

My soul magnifies the Lord!
The Lord is coming
to save his people;
Mary's obedience
and God's willingness
are his precious gift to us.

My soul magnifies the Lord!

Confession

You have done so much, dear
  Lord,
and we so little in return.
You ask for humility
and we are often a proud
  people.
You ask for willingness
and we are often a stubborn
  people.
You ask for repentance
and we are often a deaf people.
You ask for service
and we are often a busy people.
You have done so much, dear
  Lord,
and we so little in return.

Forgive us, we humbly pray.
Teach us obedience,
that we, like Mary,
might be your willing servants;
that through the ordinary
  people
gathered here today
the extraordinary might be
  achieved for you.

Thanksgiving

You did not throw this earth
into the vastness of the
  universe
as if by chance.
It was your hand
that placed it there,
your plan to grow it there.

You did not populate this earth
with a people reflecting your
  image
as if by chance.
It was your will
that brought us here,
your breath that keeps us here.

You did not come to walk this
  earth
and journey from stable to
  cruel cross
as if by chance.
It was your love
that took you there,
your grace that draws us near.

Thank you, Lord,
for your constant
and deliberate
care.

Year C

Christmas Day

ISAIAH 52:7–10; PSALM 98; HEBREWS 1:1–4 [5–12]; JOHN 1:1–14

Opening prayer

To some, today means
gifts beneath a tree
and Santa's little helper.

To us, it means
a humble stable,
a loving mother
and the birth of a Saviour.
A day of joy,
a day of wonder,
a day to offer
not gifts that bring
temporary pleasure,
but hearts that join
the heavenly chorus
resounding through this world
with Hallelujahs.

Adoration

The crowds were elsewhere
when you were born, dear
  Lord,
and this was a precious
  moment
between two parents
and the angelic host,
for there must have been
such rejoicing in heaven
when your first cry was heard!
What a joy for those shepherds
to be ushered through the
  door,
and what a joy for us,
gathered here today
to welcome, in our own way,
the Saviour of this world.

Confession

It is easy
on this of all days
to remember the moment
the divine touched this fragile
  earth
and, in humility,
uttered his first cry.

It is harder
in our daily lives
to remember the moment
you touched our fragile hearts
and with graceful love
caused us to cry,
'My Lord, and my God!'

Forgive us,
and draw us back
to the stable door
in our daily journeying,
that we might remember
the day the divine touched
  earth and hearts.

Thanksgiving

Rejoice and give thanks!
This is a day of celebration
as once more the Creator
walks within the garden
as in Eden long ago,
the love of God
in frail human flesh
reaching out in welcome.
This is a day of celebration:
Rejoice and give thanks!

Year C

First Sunday of Christmas

Sunday between 26 December and 1 January

1 SAMUEL 2:18–20, 26; PSALM 148; COLOSSIANS 3:12–17; LUKE 2:41–52

Opening prayer

A lot has happened in the last
week. Some of us have spent time
travelling to visit family and old
friends. Gifts and greetings have
been exchanged; carols have been
sung to remind us of the birth of
the Christ-child. Now a sense of
'normality' is being felt again in
our lives.

In our Gospel reading we find
a different Jesus from the one we
left on Christmas morning. He
has survived Herod's hunt for the
firstborn in Bethlehem and has
been quietly growing up in and
around the carpenter's shop in
Nazareth.

Father God, the Christmas story
did not end in the stable but
continued as Jesus grew to be a
man, unnoticed by the world,
apart from his appearance at the
temple, his spiritual home on
earth. As we close the pages of
one year and begin the next, may
we grow in faith and wisdom,
closer to you each and every day.

Adoration

For the joy of your
  presence,
changing and renewing us
day by day,
we offer you our praise.

For the blessing you bring
  us,
the outpouring of your love
day by day,
we offer you our praise.

For peace beyond
  understanding,
blessed assurance
day by day,
we offer you our praise.

For the word that endures,
teaching and challenging us
day by day,
we offer you our praise

Confession

Saviour God, how easy it is to
  forget
the joy of Christmas morning
in the bustle of the moment,
when pressures of this world
obscure our vision of the next.
How easy it is to forget the gift
so undeserved and free,
when cards and baubles
are packed away
and thank-you letters sent.
Forgive our short memories,
and, as one year leads to next,
lead us on to new adventures
as we walk with you
day by day.

Thanksgiving

God of the journey from year
  to year,
we offer you our thanks
for the patience you have
  shown us
at the start of each new day;
for the blessings you still offer
when we don't know what to
  pray;
for the grace that you extend
  to us
even when we turn away.

God of the journey from year
  to year,
we stand in need of grace.
Take the imperfect that we are
and use us as your hands;
take the words we try to say
so some might understand
that love came down at
  Christmas
to bring God's grace to us,
and walked a path we follow
toward a promised land.

Year C

Second Sunday of Christmas

Sunday between 2 and 5 January

JEREMIAH 31:7–14; PSALM 147:12–20; EPHESIANS 1:3–14; JOHN 1:[1–9] 10–18

Opening prayer

There's something wonderful
in the thought that the one
who brought this world into
existence loves us enough
to want to call us sons and
daughters.

Father God, as we join
together in worship today, we
do so in the certain knowledge
that you have called us into
your family, so that we may
know you better, experience
your love and know the
blessing that comes from being
in your presence.

Adoration

Creator God, who loves us
more than we can know,
who has chosen us
to be family,
we praise your holy name.

Jesus Christ, Son of God,
Word become flesh
dwelling among us,
sacrificed for us,
we praise your holy name.

Holy Spirit, breath of life,
power within us
from the moment
we first believed,
we praise your holy name.

Confession

God of the journey,
your invitation is to follow you
without fear of stumbling;
your arm is strong enough
to steady the weakest soul.

God of the journey,
grant us faith enough
to take you at your word,
and, should we struggle,
may we know you're with us
 in our walk.

God of the journey,
forgive our times of doubt,
and, drawing close to us,
fill these hearts with love
so we may sing your praise.

Thanksgiving

Gracious God, we thank you
that we were a chosen people
before the creation of this
 world.
Chosen by adoption as sons
and daughters of our heavenly
 Father
through the love of Christ
poured out upon a cross.
Chosen that we might live
holy and blameless lives
and that your name might be
 lifted high.
Chosen that we might know
the hope to which we are
 called,
a promise of eternal life.
Chosen that by your Spirit
we might draw others in
and the whole earth
might live to sing your praise.

Gracious God, we thank you
that we are a chosen people.

The Epiphany

6 January or first Sunday in January

ISAIAH 60:1–6; PSALM 72:[1–7] 10–14; EPHESIANS 3:1–12; MATTHEW 2:1–12

Opening prayer

The story is out! Jesus Christ,
the light of the world, has been
born to dispel the darkness
that covers its people. God's
glory appears in human form.
Life on earth will never be the
same again.

Father God, the star that
led the magi to the stable
announced to the world that
its Saviour was born. Today
we live in a world that is still
covered by darkness, still
needing to make that journey
to the stable door. May our
lives reflect your light day
by day as we seek to serve
wherever you have placed us,
so that we might be the means
through which others can
encounter Jesus Christ.

Adoration

Arise, shine, for the light of the
world has come.
Darkness covers the earth and
its people
but the radiance of God's light
burns away its shadows,
illuminates the smallest corner
and heralds the start
of a new day.

Hearts need no longer fear;
souls can be set free;
one shall follow another,
nation follow nation,
and kings and princes bow
down in awe
before the one who comes to
reign.

Arise, shine, for the light of the
world has come.
Hallelujah!

Confession

We stand at your feet,
  Lord God,
creation facing its creator,
hearts laid bare by your light,
humbly asking for mercy.
We come as a people in need
of assurance and forgiveness.
We come as a people in need
of healing and wholeness.
We come dependent upon
  your grace.

Draw close to us.
Enfold us in your arms.
Fill us with your Spirit,
that we might reflect your light
in this dark world,
speak your word with boldness
and draw others to your feet.

Thanksgiving

Heavenly Father, thank you
that for those who seek a
  Saviour,
we lead them to the stable,
to the one who was born
to bring salvation,
healing and liberty.

Thank you
that for those who seek
  assurance,
we lead them to the light,
to the one who opens eyes
to understand
your word and truth.

Thank you
that for those who seek
  forgiveness,
we lead them to a love
beyond comprehension,
to wholeness,
mercy and grace.

Baptism of Christ

Sunday between 7 and 13 January

ISAIAH 43:1–7; PSALM 29; ACTS 8:14–17; LUKE 3:15–17, 21–22

Opening prayer

We sometimes forget that
the Jesus whose birth we
celebrated at Christmas spent
many years growing up in a
small Jewish family. He would
grow wiser and stronger,
learning a trade, waiting for
his moment, waiting for the
pieces of the bigger picture to
fall into place. Then he would
enter the waters of the Jordan,
see the Holy Spirit descend on
him and hear the voice from
heaven proclaiming, 'You are
my one dear Son; in you I take
great delight.'

Father God, as we join
together in worship, let us not
forget your infinite patience
and love in dealing with your
people, among whom we
count ourselves. Use us in your
service, that we might draw
others into your kingdom, to
your praise and glory.

Adoration

The God who breathed this
    world alive
and sustains it day by day,
whose hands threw planets
    into orbit
and controls our destiny,
says, 'Do not be afraid, for I am
    with you.'

The God who fills the ocean
    depths
and sets tides on their way,
who causes mountains to be
    raised
and rainbows to span the sky,
says, 'I have called you by
    name, you are mine.'

The God who made this fertile
    earth
and seed to sow within,
whose artistry creates
    butterflies
and the early morning dew,
says, 'You are precious in my
    sight.'

Confession

Your majesty is beyond
imagination,
the eternal king,
high and lifted up,
whom the angels worship.

Your power is beyond
understanding,
the Creator God
who shakes the heavens,
yet holds us in his hands.

Your mercy is beyond
our deserving,
the Saviour God
once born for us,
now sacrificed in love.

Forgive the smallness
of our faith,
the magnitude
of our need,
the depth
of our sorrow.
Raise us up to new life
and new ways of service,
through Jesus Christ
your Son, our Lord.

Thanksgiving

For John the Baptist,
preparing the way by
    repentance and baptism,
we thank you.

For Jesus Christ,
proclaimed your Son by water
    and Spirit,
we thank you.

For good news
that salvation has come to the
    earth,
we thank you.

For your love,
undeserved and graciously
    given,
we thank you.

For the Holy Spirit,
transforming and empowering
    lives,
we thank you.

For your promise
of an eternity in which to
    praise you,
we thank you.

Year C

Second Sunday of Epiphany

Sunday between 14 and 20 January

ISAIAH 62:1–5; PSALM 36:5–10; 1 CORINTHIANS 12:1–11; JOHN 2:1–11

Opening prayer

In our worship today, let us
remember that the love of
God for his people and for his
church knows no limits. The
psalmist talks of God's love
reaching up to the heavens
and his justice to the depth of
the ocean, and yet God blesses
us as individuals with the gifts
of his Spirit so that his church,
his people, might be a light in
this place to his glory.

Father God, we bring our
offering of worship and, with
it, the service of our lives
through this coming week.
May we go from this place
knowing that we have met
with you and been blessed by
your Spirit, to live and work to
your glory.

Adoration

God, whose love reaches to the
    highest heavens,
how can we keep silent?
God, whose righteousness
    stands like the tallest
    mountain,
how can we keep silent?
God, whose justice is deeper
    than any ocean,
how can we keep silent?
God, whose grace flows like a
    never ending river,
how can we keep silent?

How can we not proclaim your
    majesty
from generation to generation?
How can we not raise the lamp
    of your salvation
for all the world to see?
God, whose love reaches to the
    highest heavens,
we lift up your mighty name!

Confession

We pray for confidence
to share your word with others
and for the opportunity to
  proclaim it.
Forgive our reluctance,
our timidity.

We pray for wisdom
to know what should be said
and the moment in which to
  say it.
Forgive our reticence,
our anxiety.

We pray for knowledge
of the fullness of your grace
and the willingness to live it.
Forgive our ignorance,
our self-reliance.

Be the centre of all we are,
the light by which we walk,
the grace by which we talk,
the blessing that we share.

Thanksgiving

For the gifts of your Spirit,
present within us
in knowledge, teaching,
wisdom, healing,
in faith that's strong,
in words and song,
we thank you, Lord.

Use them in this place
and build us up, Lord,
for in your power
lives are transformed,
in your power
lives are made new,
in your power
your church is revived
and your name is lifted high.

For the gifts of your Spirit,
present within us,
we thank you, Lord

Third Sunday of Epiphany

Sunday between 21 and 27 January

NEHEMIAH 8:1–3, 5–6, 8–10; PSALM 19; 1 CORINTHIANS 12:12–31A; LUKE 4:14–21

Opening prayer

Lord God, we are here today
to listen to your word,
bring the prayers that are
  on our hearts
and join together in
  fellowship.
Speak to us through scripture,
hymns, prayer and
  meditation.
Grant us ears to hear,
hearts to listen
and lives prepared for service.

Adoration

Leader: The heavens declare
  your glory
**All: And the skies proclaim your
handiwork.**

Morning sun and moon by
  night,
the light and warmth that fuel
  our life:

Leader: The heavens declare
  your glory
**All: And the skies proclaim your
handiwork.**

Rolling hills and mountain peak,
flowing stream and ocean deep:

Leader: The heavens declare
  your glory
**All: And the skies proclaim your
handiwork.**

Thunder's roar and gentle rain,
creation sings its song of praise:

Leader: The heavens declare
  your glory
**All: And the skies proclaim your
handiwork.**

Opening Prayer. 276

Verse

Hymn MP 77 Christ Triumphant
ever reigning

Prayer

Hymn MP ~~MP~~ ~~MP~~ 93 MP
Come let us join
our cheerful Songs

Notices

Bible Reading

Hymn — MP 202 Hail the day
that sees
Him rise.

Talk

Hymn — MP 426 Look ye
saints

Benediction

Confession

You speak to us in many ways,
through rushing wind
or still small voice,
in scripture's word
or through your grace.
And we in turn find many
  ways
to hear the world's
insistent voice
break through
and take your place.

Forgive the frailty of our faith.
Help us hear your voice
above the clamour of this
  world,
recognise the difference
and follow only you.

Thanksgiving

Generous God, for all that
  sustains us,
air to breathe, warmth and
  light,
food to eat, water to drink,
we gratefully offer our songs
  and praise.

Holy God, for your Spirit who
  joins us,
one people, one body
empowered for service,
we gratefully offer our hands
  and feet.

Saving God, for your love that
  inspires us,
healing and wholeness,
freedom and justice,
we gratefully offer our hearts
  and souls.

Fourth Sunday of Epiphany

Sunday between 28 January and 3 February

JEREMIAH 1:4–10; PSALM 71:1–6; 1 CORINTHIANS 13:1–13; LUKE 4:21–30

Opening prayer

You have loved us from the
  moment we were conceived,
and your love has gathered us
  here today.
Bless our meeting together,
our worship and prayer,
the understanding of your
  word
and our going into the world.
Through our words and lives
may others be drawn into the
  arms of your love,
and the whole earth begin to
  sing your praise.

Adoration

Gracious God,
it was always your desire
that we should gather here,
bringing this offering
of adoration and praise,
for since eternity began
you have been drawing
all of creation
into your embrace.

Such love, such grace,
that touched even these souls.
For in our travelling
we saw a light that shone
straight into our hearts.

Such light, such warmth,
that brought us to our
  Saviour's feet.
And Simeon's words became
  our own,
for our eyes *have* seen your
  salvation—
a light in the nation of Israel
for all the world to see.
Gracious God,
for love that brought us here
and love that sets us free,
we lift your name on high.

Confession

Forgive us, Lord,
when we forget
where the strength
we need comes from,
and in our weakness
find we're struggling
to maintain our faith.
Remind us, Lord,
you are the strength
on whom we can call,
the power to endure,
the answer we seek,
the one in whose arms
we can safely rest.
Forgive us, Lord
when we forget.

Thanksgiving

Your love
flows like a stream
into the ocean of your grace.

Your love
encircles this world,
displaying your faithfulness.

Your love
is patient and kind,
bringing wholeness and true
  peace.

Your love
is all we desire
to heal our brokenness.

As all things pass
and fade away,
love remains
eternally.

Thank you,
Lord of love.

Year C

Proper 1

Sunday between 4 and 10 February
(if earlier than Second Sunday before Lent)
ISAIAH 6:1–8 [9–13]; PSALM 138; 1 CORINTHIANS 15:1–11; LUKE 5:1–11

Opening prayer

Reveal yourself, gracious God,
within this time of worship.
Speak to us through the songs
  we sing,
prayers we speak, words we
  hear.

Reveal yourself, gracious God,
within your family here.
In our speaking and listening,
tears and laughter, love is
  shared.

Reveal yourself, gracious God,
within these coming days,
in the places where we live,
with people we meet, at work
  and play.

Adoration

This earth, full of your glory,
praises your name
through unspoken words of
  beauty and peace;
reveals your love
through hand of stranger and
  gift of grace.

This earth, full of your glory,
praises your provision
through living water and food
  to eat;
reveals your word
through daily blessings and
  bread of life.

This earth, full of your glory,
praises your name.

Confession

If we have failed to recognise
  your love
in the actions of a friend or
  stranger,
forgive us.

If we have failed to recognise
  your voice
through the chatter of the
  world we live in,
forgive us.

If we have failed to remember
  your love
in the interactions of our daily
  life,
forgive us.

Renew our hearts in worship.
Renew our minds in wisdom.
Renew our hands in service
and may our lives become
a willing offering to you.

Thanksgiving

You challenge us to follow you,
not by staying where we are
but by stepping out in faith,
casting our net into deeper
  water,
as did Simon Peter, fisherman.

You challenge us to trust you
and be prepared for all
eventualities,
even when the load is heavy
and the journey hard.

But with your challenge
comes blessing,
as flimsy nets are filled
and broken lives made whole,
as emptiness
  becomes abundance.

Thank you for this challenge.
Grant us faith enough to
  follow
and strength enough to
  endure.
Through Christ alone we ask.

Year C

Proper 2

Sunday between 11 and 17 February
(if earlier than Second Sunday before Lent)

JEREMIAH 17:5–10; PSALM 1; 1 CORINTHIANS 15:12–20; LUKE 6:17–26

Opening prayer

Be with us Lord, in our
  singing,
our prayers and meditation,
and as we meet together
bless and encourage us,
that we might become
a blessing for those outside
  these walls.

Adoration

You are our fortress
and defender,
our protector from the storm,
in whom we take refuge
until the calm descends.

You are our foundation,
the solid rock
in whom our confidence rests.

You are justice,
compassion,
love
and peace.
You are the
everything
that fills our emptiness.

Confession

When faith is tested to the limit
and we stumble,
forgive us.

When feet stray from the path
and we wander,
forgive us.

When our neighbour is in need
and we walk by,
forgive us.

When the voices of this world
drown out your whisper,
forgive us.

When love draws us to
  your feet
in repentance,
forgive us.

Thanksgiving

Leader: God of love
**All: You are worthy of our
  thanks.**

For love that offers
  refreshment
to all who drink of it,
light to all who walk in it,
strength to all who hope in it:

Leader: God of love
**All: You are worthy of our
  thanks.**

For love that offers healing
to all who have need of it,
wholeness to all who live in it,
blessing to all who give of it:

Leader: God of love
**All: You are worthy of our
  thanks.**

Year C

Proper 3

Sunday between 18 and 24 February
(if earlier than Second Sunday before Lent)

GENESIS 45:3–11, 15; PSALM 37:1–11, 39–40; 1 CORINTHIANS 15:35–38, 42–50;
LUKE 6:27–38

Opening prayer

God of yesterday, today and
for ever, we thank you for
your loving care, protection
and strength. As Joseph, once
abandoned into slavery, was
able with confidence to state
that every part of his life was
lived according to your will, so
we ask that the whole of our
lives might be testament to
your eternal love, mercy and
grace.

Adoration

Alpha and Omega,
beginning and end
of all things,
Creator,
Sustainer,
Provider,
in your name we gather
and at your feet we bow.

Shield and defender,
tower of refuge
for the weary,
Deliverer,
Redeemer,
Forgiver,
in your name we worship
and at your feet we bow.

Confession

Let us be still before the Lord;
rest quietly in his presence;
listen.
(Pause)

Let us bring before the Lord
words that may have hurt
  others,
encouragements left unsaid,
the anger we have felt,
resentment we have fed.
Let us be still before the Lord;
rest quietly in his presence;
listen.
(Pause)

The Lord is slow to anger,
willing to forgive,
full of grace.
(Pause)

Draw near to him;
rest quietly in his presence;
listen.

Thanksgiving

God the Father,
Creator and Provider,
delighting in the lives of all
who live in grateful obedience
  to your will,
we bring to you the thanks-
  offering of our hearts.

God the Son,
Saviour and Redeemer,
welcoming all who, in
  humility,
come to you willingly as
  servants and disciples,
we bring to you the thanks-
  offering of our hands.

God the Spirit,
Power and Upholder,
living water flowing into all
who are open to the possibility
  of new birth,
we bring to you the thanks-
  offering of our lives.

Second Sunday before Lent

ISAIAH 55:10–13; PSALM 92:1–4, 12–15; 1 CORINTHIANS 15:51–58

Opening prayer

As we come together in
  worship
we join a heavenly chorus
who night and day sing out,
'Holy, holy, holy
is the Lord God Almighty,
who was, and is, and is to
  come.'
For you, Lord, are worthy
to receive glory, honour
and the praises of our hearts
and voices,
this day and all days.

Adoration

It is a thought so wonderful,
beyond our understanding,
that the God who formed the
  heavens
and within them placed this
  world,
clothed in such beauty,
seeded with life
and breath
and expectation,
should daily provide for those
who live upon its shores.

Creator God, we praise you
for such abundant provision
of water, grain
and all that we require for life.
Gracious God, you love us
more than we could know,
feeding body, soul and spirit,
building a people to call
  your own.

Shout to the Lord, all the
  earth;
let us sing the glory of his
  name!

Confession

God of grace,
forgive our ingratitude
for the blessings we have received.
Help us live the faith we proclaim.

God of peace,
forgive our impatience
with the actions of our neighbour.
Help us live the faith we proclaim.

God of love,
forgive our intolerance
toward those of other faiths or
  none.
Help us live the faith we proclaim.

God of mercy,
forgive our reluctance
to follow where your feet might
  tread.
Help us live the faith we proclaim.

God of hope,
accept our repentance
as a sacrificial offering.
Help us bring glory to your name.

Thanksgiving

Where your love resides,
there is wholeness;
where your peace inhabits,
there is harmony;
where your Spirit lives,
there is liberty.

God of gentle whisper,
cooling breeze,
green pastures
and sweet perfume,
infuse our lives
with all that is good
and pure and holy,
and we shall bring a
fragrant offering
of thanks and praise,
wherever we might be.

Sunday Next before Lent

EXODUS 34:29–35; PSALM 99; 2 CORINTHIANS 3:12—4:2; LUKE 9:28–36 [37–43]

Opening prayer

We meet today, Lord God,
not as in the days of Moses
when a physical barrier, the
veil, separated the people from
your presence, but in the sure
knowledge that when your
Son died on the cross for us,
the curtain of the temple was
torn in two, granting us access
to the holiest place.

It is in this confidence that
we approach your throne
with our sacrifice of worship,
asking that you will bless us
with your presence, draw close
to us and enable us to know
more of you.

Adoration

Awesome one, Creator of all,
the light of your glory
fills the heavens;
the breath of your Spirit
blows through the skies;
stars above stand silent witness
to the power of our God.

By your word all things were
	made;
by your breath are all
	sustained.
By your hand we were
	moulded
as a potter moulds the clay,
formed from earthly dust
into an image of the divine.
By your grace we stand here,
your creation worshipping its
	creator
with a sacrifice of praise.

Year C

Confession

For those days when we forget
how close you are
and how welcome is our
  prayer:

Leader: In your mercy
All: Forgive us.

When life distracts, our focus
  shifts
and we prefer
to listen to this world's call:

Leader: In your mercy
All: Forgive us.

When our worship fails to
  please you
because our lives
do not reflect the words we
  use:

Leader: In your mercy
All: Forgive us.

Embrace us again, dear Lord,
in loving fellowship with you.
Draw us closer to your throne
and reveal yourself once more.

Thanksgiving

Almighty Father,
beginning and end of all
  we are,
the hope to which we cling,
to you we bring our sacrifice
  of thanks.

Jesus Christ,
Word of God becoming flesh,
in whose footsteps we now
  tread,
to you we bring our sacrifice
  of thanks.

Holy Spirit,
creating breath and life for all,
living presence within our
  hearts,
to you we bring our sacrifice
  of thanks.

Three in One,
be the unity between our lives,
the light by which we see
and the rock upon which
  we walk,
today and all days.

First Sunday of Lent

DEUTERONOMY 26:1–11; PSALM 91:1–2, 9–16; ROMANS 10:8B–13; LUKE 4:1–13

Opening prayer

Today we meet to declare our
  faith
in God the Father, Creator
  of all,
in God the Son, our Saviour
  and Lord,
in God the Spirit, three in one.
Today we meet to praise
  our God.

Adoration

Leader: For the blessings of
  each day
All: We praise your holy name.

For strength to endure
in times of distress,
shelter from storm,
and your arms to protect.

Leader: For the blessings of
  each day
All: We praise your holy name.

For footsteps to follow
with you as our guide,
and grace that will show
through our actions and words.

Leader: For the blessings of
  each day
All: We praise your holy name.

For faith to believe
and a heart filled with hope,
your presence beside us
from the moment we wake.

Leader: For the blessings of
  each day
All: We praise your holy name.

Confession

You call us to follow
and our footsteps falter;
you hold out your hand
and we treat you as a stranger;
you whisper our name
and we simply ignore you.
Gracious God,
slow to anger,
swift to bless,
  forgive us,
    restore us.

Grant us hearts that stand firm,
a faith that is strong
and a hope that endures,
that we might become
willing servants
of our heavenly king,
and your glory and praise
may be the song that we sing.

Thanksgiving

Sometimes you lead us
by your Spirit
into wilderness places
where faith is tested,
but you do not leave us
on our own.

Sometimes you lead us
by your Spirit
into difficult places
where words are required,
but it's *your* voice that's heard,
not our own.

Sometimes you lead us
by your Spirit
into desolate places
where comfort is needed,
but *your* hands bring peace,
not our own.

For the places you lead us
and the Spirit you give us,
we bring this offering of
  thanks.

Second Sunday of Lent

GENESIS 15:1–12, 17–18; PSALM 27; PHILIPPIANS 3:17—4:1; LUKE 9:28–36

Opening prayer

We come together to worship
the God of Abraham, the God
of Jacob and the God of David.
We worship the one true God,
creator of all, Lord of all, our
strength and hope, our light
and our salvation. We come
together as family, joined
by the hands of fellowship,
brothers and sisters of our
heavenly Father.

Adoration

What more could we ask
than to gaze upon your beauty
with eyes and heart of faith
as we journey on with you?
In times of plenty
and times of want,
in lofty places and low,
you keep us safe,
secure from harm.

What more could we ask
than to gaze upon your beauty
with eyes of vision and hope
as we journey on with you?
In times of doubt
and fragile faith,
in suffering and pain,
you hold us tight.
What can we fear?

What more could we ask
than to gaze upon your
    beauty?

Confession

The path we walk
is often strewn
with distractions
that cause us to stumble.

Leader: Teach us your way,
O Lord
**All: And we shall follow in
your footsteps.**

The path we walk
is often chosen
with little thought
of the destination.

Leader: Teach us your way,
O Lord
**All: And we shall follow in
your footsteps.**

The path we walk
is often clouded
with lack of faith
and indecision.

Leader: Teach us your way,
O Lord
**All: And we shall follow in
your footsteps.**

Thanksgiving

With your presence beside us,
who can stumble?
You lead us from darkness
to brighter places,
brand new days
and opportunities.

With your presence beside us,
who can stumble?
You bring us from familiar
to exciting places,
replacing fear
with possibilities.

With your presence beside us,
who can stumble?
You lead us to shelter
in tranquil places
during life's storms
and adversities.

For your presence,
your guidance,
your shelter,
we thank you, Lord.

Third Sunday of Lent

ISAIAH 55:1–9; PSALM 63:1–11; 1 CORINTHIANS 10:1–13; LUKE 13:1–9

Opening prayer

This is the day the Lord has
  made;
let us rejoice in all that he has
  given.
Come as the hungry, to feed
  on his word.
Come as the thirsty, to drink of
  his love.
Come as the faithful, to
  worship the Lord.
This is the day the Lord has
  made;
let us rejoice in all that he has
  given.

Adoration

Faithful Father, whose love
  flows
as a river over parched land,
refreshing and reviving.

Precious Son, word of life
to those who thirst for truth
in a world awash with lies.

Gracious Spirit, gentle breeze,
strength and comfort
for hearts that are dry.

Triune God, blessed one,
the unity to which we hold,
living water,
bread of life,
to you we bring our praise.

Confession

When our hearts are willing
but our minds confused
by the world in which we
  move,
forgive us.

When our souls are thirsty
and we drink the water
that so easily runs dry,
forgive us.

May we seek your face
in a world that passes you by;
may we hear your voice
in a world focused on 'I';
may we know your mercy
and share it on our journey
this and every day.

Thanksgiving

In a world beset with conflict,
you are the enduring peace,
a heart of love that beats
in the souls of all who confess
  your name.

Leader: God of love
**All: We bring our grateful
  thanks.**

In a world beset with doubt,
you are waiting to be found,
the living water that
refreshes all who ask the
  question 'How?'

Leader: God of love
**All: We bring our grateful
  thanks.**

In a world beset with sin,
you are mercy and grace
that is freely offered
to all who hold their hands out
  to receive.

Leader: God of love
**All: We bring our grateful
  thanks.**

Fourth Sunday in Lent

JOSHUA 5:9–12; PSALM 32; 2 CORINTHIANS 5:16–21; LUKE 15:1–3, 11B–32

Opening prayer

We worship you, God of
promise, whose saving
grace brought a people
from captivity into a land of
promise, and whose enduring
love still leads us from places
of captivity into peace,
forgiveness and eternal life.
Your promises endure for ever.
Your promises will be fulfilled.

Adoration

God of the journey,
of new beginnings,
provision,
direction
and destination,
we praise your glorious name.

God of the journey,
of new creation,
wholeness,
forgiveness,
reconciliation,
we praise your glorious name.

God of the journey,
of new possibility,
service,
blessing
and thanksgiving,
we praise your glorious name.

Confession

Grant us a willingness
to say 'sorry'
and a heart for repentance.

Grant us a childlikeness
to accept your word
and know forgiveness.

Grant us a humbleness
to start anew
and put the past behind us.

God of grace and mercy,
be the new beginning
that starts with our repentance
and leads us into tomorrow.

Thanksgiving

How can we thank the one
  who forgives,
loves and accepts us,
who will not reject us?

With the offering of our hearts,
the service of our lives
and a sacrifice of praise.

How can we thank the one
  who loves us,
laid down his life for us,
heals and restores us?

With our attitude to others,
the compassion we show
and a faith that grows.

Fifth Sunday of Lent

ISAIAH 43:16–21; PSALM 126; PHILIPPIANS 3:4B–14; JOHN 12:1–8

Opening prayer

In our fellowship together,
our singing and our prayer,
we hear your voice
whisper into our lives,
'See, I am doing a new thing!'
God of new beginnings,
grant us a new heart for
  worship,
a new heart for your people,
a new love for our neighbour
and a new willingness for
  service,
that your name might be
  lifted high
in this place and in these lives.

Adoration

To know you, Lord—
what more could we desire?
To know your love,
hear your call,
feel your touch,
understand your suffering,
and follow where you have
  walked
into resurrection life.

To know you, Lord—
what more could we desire?
To run the race,
eyes focused,
Spirit-filled,
stumbling but rising up,
heading toward the glorious
  eternity
of resurrection life.

Confession

Forgive us when we tire
of the journey
and wander from the path,
when our heart is set
not on the goal
but on some distant shore
that offers only temporary
  respite.

Forgive us when the light
that once shone
within our soul is dimmed,
when our love
is not focused on the Saviour
but on satisfaction of self,
which leads to an altogether
different destination.

Forgive;
  restore;
    refocus;
      revive;
reignite the flame within,
that we might illuminate
  the way
that so many seek to travel.
Through Jesus Christ alone,
  we ask.

Thanksgiving

Lord, we offer this prayer
of thanksgiving
as a fragrant offering
rising from grateful hearts
into your glorious presence.

May it be
an offering of thanks
for love poured out
so we might be set free.

May it be
an offering of thanks
for strength and faith
in our daily journeying.

May it be
an offering of thanks
transformed by grace
into service, Lord, for you.

Palm Sunday

LITURGY OF THE PALMS: PSALM 118:1–2, 19–29; LUKE 19:28–40

LITURGY OF THE PASSION: ISAIAH 50:4–9A; PSALM 31:9–16; PHILIPPIANS 2:5–11; LUKE 22:14—23:56

Opening prayer

We meet together
in the presence of a God
whose love is freedom,
whose touch is healing,
whose voice is peace.

Lord, your Spirit is with us
as we join in worship;
your Spirit is with us
as we join in service.

May your love bring freedom,
your touch bring healing
and your voice be the peace
that we take from this place
and share with all we meet
though the coming days,
that your name alone
might be glorified.

Adoration

Hosanna!
Hosanna in the highest!
The cry goes up from earth
 to sky
and angelic voices echo
 the refrain—
a heavenly chorus,
a paean of praise
to the one who comes
in the name of the Lord.

Hosanna!
Hosanna in the highest!
Blessed are you, Son of God,
riding triumphantly to
 the cross—
a sacrifice
and a gift of life
to the one who kneels
at the feet of the Lord.

Hosanna!
Hosanna in the highest!

Confession

When pride
and selfishness
obscure our vision,
and voices
of this world
confuse our mission,
let your will,
not ours, be done.

Be the centre,
the focus
of all we are.
Be the one
we depend upon.
In all the decisions
that we shall make,
let your will,
not ours, be done.

Thanksgiving

To those who hunger,
you are the bread of life.
To those who thirst,
you are a refreshing stream.
To those who mourn,
you are a hand to hold.
To those in need,
you are an untiring friend.
To those who question,
you are the one they seek.
To those who are blind,
you are their guiding feet.
To those who ask,
you are the Son of God.
To those who kneel,
you are the forgiving king.

We give you thanks
for all that you are
to us.

Year C

Good Friday

ISAIAH 52:12—53:12; PSALM 22; HEBREWS 10:16–25 [HEBREWS 4:14–16; 5:7–9]; JOHN 18:1—19:42

Opening prayer

God of love,
in a moment of quietness
we remember the reason we
  are here.
(Pause)

God of grace,
in a moment of quietness
we remember the greatest gift
  of all.
(Pause)

God of love and grace,
in this time together
be the blessing that we receive
  today.

Adoration

For God so loves the world
that he creates us in his image,
to partner with creation
and keep it in our care.

For God so loves the world
that he rescues us from
  captivity,
and leads us through our
  wilderness
into a promised land.

For God so loves the world
that he gives his all, opens up
  his heart,
journeys to a cross
and stretches wide his arms
for us to gather safely within.

Confession

Gracious God, forgive us
when we fail to understand
the depth of sorrow
you must have felt
as your people once again
rejected the one who
  made them.
(Pause)

Gracious God, forgive us
when we fail to understand
the depth of love
that sought to bring
a rebellious children
back into their Father's
  loving arms.
(Pause)

Gracious God, forgive us
when we fail to understand
the depth of your grace,
that opens wide
the gates of heaven for all
who accept this gift and
  enter in.
(Pause)

Thanksgiving

The journey began
with a hero's welcome,
Hallelujahs,
palm branches,
cheering crowds,
and temple cleansed.
It ended with
a friend's betrayal,
jeering crowds,
crown of thorns,
spilling of blood,
rejection.

For the mystery
of salvation,
and a Saviour
holding out his arms
in welcome,
we give you thanks.

Easter Day

ACTS 10:34–43; PSALM 118:1–2, 14–24; 1 CORINTHIANS 15:19–26; JOHN 20:1–18

Opening prayer

This is the day when we
acknowledge the truth of
the resurrection and all that
it means to us. This is the
day when we join with the
psalmist and proclaim, 'The
Lord has become my salvation.
I will not die but live, and will
proclaim what he has done!'

Resurrection God, we raise our
  voices
and hands to you in worship,
for the great mystery of your
  love for us,
for the necessary sadness of
  Good Friday
and for the hope that Easter
  brings.
Speak to us through your word
and the hymns and songs we
  sing,
that this place may resound
  with joy.

Adoration

Hallelujah!
Jesus is risen!
He is risen indeed!

May this declaration
resound not only in these walls
but in the lives
of all we meet.
May it for ever be
the truth of which we speak.
Your love,
once sown within a garden,
tended for your own people,
neglected and rejected,
now spreads its sweet perfume
in this place
and wherever it is shown.

Hallelujah!
Jesus is risen!
He is risen indeed!

Confession

When our faith
stands at the grave,
grieving
for a stone that's rolled away,
forgive us.

When our faith
is short of
understanding,
though the truth is there to
  see,
forgive us.

When our faith,
beset by doubt, sees
no further
than an empty tomb today,
forgive us.

Bring to mind
the cry of Mary,
'I have seen the Lord!'
and grant us faith to believe.

Thanksgiving

We thank you
that Easter is not about
a people,
but *all* people,
that your love
and your salvation
are for all who confess
with voices, hearts and lives
that the tomb is empty.
Jesus is risen,
that we might know
forgiveness,
that many might be
reborn
and your name
be glorified
now and for eternity.

Second Sunday of Easter

ACTS 5:27–32; PSALM 118:14–29; REVELATION 1:4–8; JOHN 20:19–31

Opening prayer

Into your presence we come,
God of grace and peace,
who was, and is,
and ever shall be
the eternal one.
In fellowship we come,
bound together in the love
that died and rose again,
our Saviour Jesus Christ.

Adoration

This world would silence your
  name
but we will not be quiet.
This world would deny your name
but we will speak it out.

God of all beginnings,
who breathed and this world
  lived,
spoke and this world moved,
loved and brought us to a garden,
a gift of grace providing for our
  needs.

God of our salvation,
who chose a people for his own,
spoke the word of life,
poured out pure love, and in a
  garden
showed the world what love
  could do.

This world would silence your
  name
but we will not be quiet.
This world would deny your name
but we will speak it out.

Confession

You call us to be your voices in
  this world
and we stay silent.
You call us to be your hands in
  this world
and we keep them hidden.
You call us to be your feet in
  this world
and we go our own way.

When we meet someone
  looking for the way
and say nothing, forgive us.
When we meet someone who
  needs your touch
and do nothing, forgive us.
When we are called to take up
  your cross
and carry nothing, forgive us.

Breathe life into these dry
  bones;
bring freedom to these lives,
that we might declare
with heart and soul and voice
that you are our Lord and
  our God.

Thanksgiving

For peace
beyond understanding—
shalom—
your desire for all
that is good and fruitful,
all that makes us whole,
we thank you.

For grace
we do not deserve,
freedom,
forgiveness for all
that is wrong in our lives
that keeps us from you,
we thank you.

For life
poured out on a cross—
salvation—
that divine mystery
of love by which all
might know you as Abba,
  Father,
we thank you.

Year C

Third Sunday of Easter

ACTS 9:1–6 [7–20]; PSALM 30; REVELATION 5:11–14; JOHN 21:1–19

Opening prayer

May the God of life, who
spoke to the heart of Saul on
the road to Damascus, speak
to us in this place as we gather
for worship, bring our prayers
and listen to his word. May
we see his light, follow where
he leads us and be used in
service, for the building up of
his church.

Adoration

Worthy are you
to receive from us
the honour and praise
that's due your name,
Lamb of God,
slain for us
to pay the price
of our sinfulness.
Now to him
who sits on the throne,
and the Lamb
who leads us home,
may praise and honour,
glory and power
be shown
for ever and ever.

Confession

You speak to us in many ways,
in the spectacular
and in a quiet whisper,
in the bustle of a street
and the solitude of a wilderness,
in the ebb and flow of daily life,
traffic jam or office desk.

You speak to us in many ways
and our ears are often attuned
to different voices,
louder, more insistent voices.

Forgive us
when we fail to hear your voice
and follow the wisdom of this
  world.
Forgive us
when we bring tears to
  your eyes.
Open our ears to hear
and our hearts to serve,
that our lives might bring
a smile to your face
and glory to your name.

Thanksgiving

For all answers to prayer,
gracious Lord, we thank you.
For a touch bringing healing
and lives made whole.
For the sharing of comfort
when the season is cold.
For one door opened
and another one closed.
For the unseen blessings
of sharing your word.
Gracious Lord, we thank you
for all answers to prayer.

Fourth Sunday of Easter

ACTS 9:36–43; PSALM 23; REVELATION 7:9–17; JOHN 10:22–30

Opening prayer

The Bible gives us a wonderful image of God as shepherd, and in some parts of the world the enduring bond between the shepherd and his sheep has changed little since biblical times. It's the dependence of the sheep on their shepherd for safety and sustenance that is the mirror of our relationship with God.

Good Shepherd, who leads us beside still waters and into green pastures, be close to us in our gathering today. May we feed on your word, know your protection and be sustained by your Spirit, this day and every day.

Adoration

God of love,
you care for us as Shepherd,
leading us to fresh pasture and
  living water.
You care for us as Father,
drawing those you love close
  into your embrace.
You care for us as Saviour,
forgiving all who draw near to
  you in faith.
You care for us as Lord and
  King,
bringing us into the heart of
  your kingdom.
God of love,
you care for us.
What greater blessing can
  there be
than this?

Confession

When we stray from the path
  you have chosen,
diverted by the promise of
  better days,
tempted by the scenery
  around us,
searching for a different way,
forgive us.
Show us the better way—
walking in your steady
  footprints,
listening to your voice that
  calls us,
feeding on your word that
  nourishes,
living our lives in grateful
  service day by day.

Thanksgiving

Praise and honour,
glory and power
belong to our God
for ever and ever.
Accept this offering today—
our thankfulness
for all that you have done
and are yet to do in our lives;
and our sacrifice,
all that we might do for you
and for those you lead us to.
Praise and honour,
glory and power
belong to our God
for ever and ever.

Year C

Fifth Sunday of Easter

ACTS 11:1–18; PSALM 148; REVELATION 21:1–6; JOHN 13:31–35

Opening prayer

Let us be still for a moment
as we draw near to worship
God. Let us remind ourselves
why we are gathered together
today. Listen. God speaks even
through the background noise
of the world around us.

Lord God, in this short time
together, open our eyes to see
your vision for this place and
our part within it. Teach us,
hear our prayers, and enable
us for service wherever you
might take us, to your praise
and glory.

Adoration

Praise the Lord, all the
  heavens;
proclaim his name from
  mountain peak and valley
  floor.
Praise the Lord, sun, moon and
  stars;
proclaim his name in summer
  skies and rainbow hue.
Praise the Lord, all creatures
  upon the earth;
proclaim his name in eagle's
  wing and lion's roar.

Praise the Lord, all rulers and
  kings;
proclaim his name who creates
  all things anew.
Praise the Lord, whether
  young or old;
proclaim his name, whose
  gracious love extends to all.

Let all things that have breath
  within them
praise the Lord.

Confession

You love us without
  questioning,
heal and bring wholeness
without prejudice,
embrace us
as a parent would their child.
Forgive us when we forget,
feel isolated and alone,
and don't know where to
  turn.
Forgive us when we fail you,
choose those we will
  minister to
and don't listen to your word.

You love us without
  questioning;
may we bring compassion,
healing and peace
without prejudice
to all whom you might lead
  us to this day.

Thanksgiving

Your commands are not
  burdensome;
your way of life is our example,
your footsteps there to be found.

'Love one another;
care for children,
brothers, sisters and outcasts.
If you are my disciples,
then show the world;
demonstrate your discipleship
and love both lovely and
  unloved.
Show God's grace to this world!'

As we open our hearts
and follow as you have shown,
others will discover you through
  our words
and by the life we share.

For the love that you have
  given us
and the blessings you have
  shown us,
we thank you, God of love and
  grace.

Sixth Sunday of Easter

ACTS 16:9–15; PSALM 67; REVELATION 21:10; 21:22—22:5; JOHN 14:23–29

Opening prayer

May peace beyond all
  understanding,
which has its source
in Father, Son and Spirit,
be with us as we meet,
to still our souls
and join our hearts as one.
May the gentle whisper
of the God of grace
speak to us through our
  worship,
the reading and understanding
  of scripture,
and be the message of our lives
as we leave this place.

Adoration

May the nations praise you;
may all the nations praise you!
You rule your people with
  justice and wisdom,
bless them with grace and
  peace
and bring a harvest where
  your seed is sown.

May the nations praise you;
may all the nations praise you!
From generation to generation
you've led your people to the
  waters of life
and to fruitfulness where your
  love is shown.

May the nations praise you;
may all the nations praise you!

Confession

Whenever self obscures the
  needs of others,
forgive us.
Whenever we forget who is
  our neighbour,
forgive us.
Whenever we pass by on the
  other side,
forgive us.
Whenever we forget to say
  'Well done!'
forgive us.
Whenever we forget the path
  we tread,
forgive us.
For all those times we bring
  sorrow to your heart,
draw us back into your
  forgiving arms
and teach us, once again, your
  way.

Thanksgiving

Leader: God of the moment
**All: We thank you for all your
  blessings.**

In the ebb and flow of daily
  life,
you shed light upon the way,
reveal the path that we should
  walk
and guide our hearts and souls
  in praise.

Leader: God of the moment
**All: We thank you for all your
  blessings.**

In the ebb and flow of daily
  life,
no darkness bars our way;
your glory shines in our hearts
  as we walk
where you would lead us
  every day.

Leader: God of the moment
**All: You thank you for all your
  blessings.**

Ascension Day

May also be used on the Seventh Sunday of Easter

ACTS 1:1–11; PSALM 47; EPHESIANS 1:15–23; LUKE 24:44–53

Opening prayer

Risen, ascended Jesus,
we gather in your name
to declare our faith
and bring our worship
to this world's Saviour,
our Lord and our King.

Adoration

When you held out your arms
upon that cruel cross
to welcome sinners home,
your time on earth was almost
  done.
Now, ascended
to your heavenly throne,
you welcome us to be the ones
through whom others might
  be drawn
to the cross, the grave and
  beyond,
to new life, a heavenly
  kingdom
and a risen, ascended king.

Hallelujah!
For the Lord our God,
the Almighty, reigns!

Confession

This world would happily
  believe
in Jesus the teacher,
Jesus the preacher,
Jesus the healer
and Jesus the revolutionary,
but not in the risen,
ascended Saviour of this world.

Forgive us, Lord,
when our own faith is troubled
and weakened
by the message of this world,
and we struggle to believe.
Be with us on our journey
as you were on the Emmaus
  road,
when you opened your
  disciples' minds
to the truth of who you are.
May we also live that truth
through our actions and words
and bring others into your
  arms.

Thanksgiving

We have a gospel to proclaim
  with thankfulness,
to spread throughout the land:
of Jesus Christ,
crucified, once dead,
now risen and ascended
and, of the church, its head.

We have a gospel to proclaim
  with thankfulness,
to spread throughout the land:
the Son of God,
now enthroned above,
still embraces the sinner
who humbly accepts his love.

Seventh Sunday of Easter

ACTS 16:16–34; PSALM 97; REVELATION 22:12–14, 16–17, 20–21; JOHN 17:20–26

Opening prayer

We meet as family in your
presence, our heavenly Father.

We meet as brothers and
sisters in Christ, accepting the
responsibility placed upon us—
to love one another as you first
loved us.

We meet as your lights in
this dark world and pray that,
through our words and our
lives, others might be drawn
into your family and accept
you as their Saviour and Lord.

Adoration

Leader: The Lord reigns.
All: Let the earth be glad!

Creator God,
breath of life,
from whom all things have
  their beginning
and unto whom all things
  return,
to Alpha and Omega we sing.

Leader: The Lord reigns.
All: Let the earth be glad!

Saviour God,
deliverer,
from whom all love has its
  beginning,
into whose arms we all are
  drawn,
to you we bring this offering.

Leader: The Lord reigns.
All: Let the earth be glad!

Confession

Heavenly Father,
we take our world for granted,
abuse its beauty and destroy
the resources that you have
  supplied for us.
Forgive us.

Heavenly Father,
we take our faith for granted,
forgetting the love and grace
  by which
your Son selflessly poured out
  his life for us.
Forgive us.

Heavenly Father,
we take your love for granted,
forgetting that walls are broken
and foundations shaken
to bring us liberty.
Forgive us.

Heavenly Father,
we take this life for granted,
ignore your path, choosing our
  way,
and, like prodigals, return to
  pray, dear Lord,
forgive us.

Thanksgiving

It is good
when children live in unity,
and your will that this is so.
Wherever there is peace,
wherever love is sown,
then your name is glorified
and your kingdom grows.

So when love is shown
in this place, we thank you.
When peace is sown
in this place, we thank you.
It is good
when children live in unity,
and your will that this should
  be so.

Year C

Day of Pentecost

ACTS 2:1–21; PSALM 104:24–34, 35B; ROMANS 8:14–17; JOHN 14:8–17 [25–27]

Opening prayer

Sovereign Lord, we meet
together to celebrate the gift
of your Holy Spirit to the
church. Bless us as we seek to
serve you today. Fill us with
your Spirit, as you filled your
followers early one morning
in Jerusalem over 2000 years
ago, that we might be your
voices, hands and presence in
the world, and draw others
into your kingdom.

Adoration

Your Spirit—
present from the beginning
of beginnings;
present in the message
of the prophets;
present in provision
for your people;
present in the life
and words of Jesus;
present in the cross
and crucifixion;
present in the lives
of the apostles;
present in the church
that you empower.

For your Spirit,
the presence of the divine
in hearts and lives,
we praise your name.

Confession

We remember the Holy Spirit,
the power in the early church,
strengthening lives,
giving courage to the
  faint-hearted,
enabling fishermen to harvest
  the world.

We remember the Holy Spirit,
the power in the lives of saints,
who offered their lives
and suffered persecution for
  the sake
of the gospel and their strong
  faith.

When we forget
the sacrifice of those who,
  by your Spirit,
spread the flame of your
  good news,
forgive us.
Fill our lives, that we might
  live for you,
speak for you
and, with courage,
stand up for you.

Thanksgiving

For the Spirit of peace
that calms our mind
and stills our life,
we give you thanks.

For the Spirit of love
that touches hearts
and reaches out,
we give you thanks.

For the Spirit of joy
that lifts our soul
and gives us faith,
we give you thanks.

For the Spirit of power,
that gift of grace
for this, your church,
we give you thanks.

Trinity Sunday

PROVERBS 8:1–4, 22–31; PSALM 8; ROMANS 5:1–5; JOHN 16:12–15

Opening prayer

Lord God, in a universe that
   is so immense,
it is easy to feel insignificant
   as we stand here today.
Yet we know that we are
   precious in your sight,
unique individuals loved
   and blessed in so many
   ways.
We stand in awe of you,
   who have created all
   things,
and we dedicate this time
   and all our days to your
   service.
Accept this offering, we
   pray,
our sacrifice of praise and
   worship.

Adoration

The warmth of the sun's embrace,
the gentle breeze swept in on the
   tide,
the rhythm of seasons,
   of new birth,
      death and re-creation,
all these speak clearly of your love,
your power and your beauty;
all are expressions of your
   creativity
and, more importantly, of yourself.
As an artist shares his personality
through each brushstroke,
so within the myriad colours
of wild flowers
you share the exuberance of
   your love.

That we can glimpse you in
   creation
tells us that you desire to be seen,
to be found and known.
Open our eyes, Lord, as we walk
   through this world,
feel the wind and sunshine,
and see the majesty of creation
   unfolding before our eyes.
Help us to see you.

Confession

God of healing,
God of wholeness,
we bring our brokenness,
our sinfulness,
our fears
and despair,
and lay them at your feet.

God of healing,
God of wholeness,
we hold out hearts and hands,
minds and souls
to feel your touch
and know the peace
that only you can bring.

God of healing,
God of wholeness,
within this precious moment
in your presence and power,
grant us the faith and
  knowledge
that, here, damaged lives
are made whole.

Thanksgiving

In the ebb and flow of daily life
you are present with us
in our journeying;
you are the peace that calms
  our souls,
the joy that fills our hearts,
the grace that overflows,
the love that draws us close.
In the ebb and flow of daily life
you are present with us
in our journeying.

For peace,
joy,
love and grace,
and the warmth of your
  embrace,
we give you thanks.

Proper 4

Sunday between 29 May and 4 June
(if after Trinity Sunday)

1 KINGS 18:20–21 [22–29] 30–39; PSALM 96; GALATIANS 1:1–12; LUKE 7:1–10

Opening prayer

Bless us as we meet together,
gracious Lord, we pray.
Bless the singing of the hymns,
the reading of your word,
the sharing of our fellowship,
the prayers that will be heard.
Bless us as we meet together,
gracious Lord, we pray.

Adoration

The heavens sing your praises,
Creator God,
and earth cries out in song.
All the works of your hands
within their beauty
sing out your name.
And we, your children,
who stand in awe
of all that you have made,
who feel so small
and yet so loved,
raise hands and hearts
and join the tuneful chorus.
The heavens sing your praises,
Creator God,
and earth cries out in song.

Confession

There are confusing voices
distracting us from your word,
persuasive voices
demanding to be heard,
drowning out the still small
  voice
we have listened to before,
bringing a new philosophy
that has no place for you.

Forgive us
when we doubt your word;
forgive us
when we are led astray.
Grant us a faith that is strong,
and wisdom to distinguish
between truth
  and that which is not.

Thanksgiving

Creator of all,
whose artistry is celebrated
in sunset glow, ocean spray
and mountain stream,
to you belongs our offering of
  thanks.

Saviour of all,
whose grace is demonstrated
in healing hands, sacrifice
and cruel cross,
to you belongs our offering of
  thanks.

Breath of life,
whose power is celebrated
in tongues of fire, living water
and lives that change,
to you belongs our offering of
  thanks.

Proper 5

Sunday between 5 and 11 June
(if after Trinity Sunday)

1 KINGS 17:8–16 [17–24]; PSALM 146; GALATIANS 1:11–24; LUKE 7:11–17

Opening prayer

In our meeting together, let
us remember that we worship
you, the God who created this
world, the God who spoke
through his prophets, led his
people from captivity to liberty,
healed the sick, fed the hungry
and was faithful even when
rejected.

You want all people to be
drawn to your love and grace,
to know your forgiveness and
the joy of your salvation. Let
us put aside all that hinders
and join together in worship
and praise.

Adoration

May the Father who is the
  source of all,
creator, sustainer and provider,
grant his blessing
on this meeting of our lives.

May the Son who gave his life
  for all,
saviour, redeemer and
  sacrifice,
be the focus
of this meeting of our lives.

May the Spirit who brings
  power to all,
knowledge, wisdom and
  flames of fire,
be the encourager
in this meeting of our lives.

May the Father, Son and
  Holy Spirit,
Godhead and glorious Trinity,
be the unity
within this meeting of our
  lives.

Confession

We are called to be your voice
in this fragile world,
to bring compassion,
peace and justice,
to comfort the weary
and speak up for the weak.
So why do we so often
see
  and fail to act;
hear
  and fail to speak;
hesitate
  before we touch?

Forgive, gracious God,
these, your reluctant disciples,
and by your Spirit
revive the life within.
Help us become the people
we ought to be.

Thanksgiving

Thank you for the gift
of sunshine and rain in due
  season,
of seed, soil and harvest,
provision for our needs
and others', if in love we share.

Thank you for the gift
of living water that does not
  run dry
and the nourishment of your
  word,
which feeds our souls
and others', if in love we share.

For love that endures,
blessings that satisfy
and the opportunity to share
all that you have given,
we bring to you our thanks.

Year C

Proper 6

Sunday between 12 and 18 June (if after Trinity Sunday)

1 KINGS 21:1–10 [11–14] 15–21A; PSALM 5:1–8; GALATIANS 2:15–21; LUKE 7:36—8:3

Opening prayer

In the meeting of our lives,
   Lord,
be the focus of all we are;
in the singing of the hymns,
the prayers that we shall make,
the reading of your word
and the preaching of the same.
In the meeting of our lives,
   Lord,
be the focus of all we are.

Adoration

Gracious God, our hearts
   cry out
in grateful praise
for all that you have done.
Your artistry
in the beauty of creation;
your faithfulness
in the leading of your people;
your wisdom
in the words and works of
   Jesus;
your salvation through
   the cross
and resurrection;
your promise
of a kingdom that is eternal.

Gracious God, our hearts
   cry out
in grateful praise.
Grant us a faith that can,
with the apostle Paul, exclaim,
'I no longer live, but Christ
   lives in me!'

Confession

You are God of justice
and God of love.
Within your nature
is the source of all forgiveness,
freedom from that which
  binds us,
and restoration of relationship.
Forgive our reluctance to let go
of the burden of our sin
and the sins of others
  against us.
Your forgiveness is total;
ours is conditional.

Help us, Lord,
not only to trust your word
and accept your forgiving love,
but to extend that grace
to those we cannot easily
  forgive,
that both they and we
might know freedom and
  release.

Thanksgiving

Thank you for all who pray
  for us;
family and friends,
and strangers who want
  nothing
but the best for us—
shalom,
peace that passes all
  understanding,
health, rest and completeness.

Thank you for listening.
Bless them as they bless us.
Thank you for the names
  and faces
that you lay upon our hearts;
we bring them to you now
in the firm knowledge
that you already have them in
  your thoughts,
and their hearts shall be
  warmed
by the *shalom* that you bring.
Thank you for listening.
Bless us as we bless them.

Year C

Proper 7

Sunday between 19 and 25 June
(if after Trinity Sunday)

1 KINGS 19:1–4 [5–7] 8–15A; PSALMS 42—43; GALATIANS 3:23–29; LUKE 8:26–39

Opening prayer

Glorious Trinity,
make your presence
known in this place
through our worship
and our prayer.
Be known by those
who would be here
but for illness
or circumstance,
that all might be blessed
by your presence,
glorious Trinity.

Adoration

God of earthquake,
wind and fire,
you reveal yourself
through the ordinary
and extraordinary,
in the day-to-day of busy lives
and in signs and wonders
that shake us to the core.
The glory of your majesty
can be heard
in the gentle whisper
of a springtime breeze,
and in an earthquake's
terrifying roar.

Let our ears and minds
be ever open to the possibility
that you are speaking to us,
and let our hearts
be attentive to your call.

Confession

This morning
and all mornings,
as we face the day
daunted by expectations
others place upon us,
weighed down by burdens,
unsure of outcomes,
opposed,
  alone,
    afraid,
remind us
that you faced this
  and more,
that we might lose
the chains that bind us,
rise above
  and beyond
the troubles of this world
and know true peace
in your embrace.

Thanksgiving

You have done so much for us,
and we have yet to tell the world
how great is our God.

May we not forget
the healing and forgiveness we
  have known.
May we not forget
your footsteps, in which we
  plant our own.
May we not forget
the seed of love that's sown
  within our hearts.
May we not forget
your mercy if we should ever
  drift apart.
May we not forget
the closeness, the warmth of
  your embrace.
May we not forget
the sacrifice you willingly made
  for us.

You have done so much for us;
may we not forget to tell the
  world, with gratitude,
how great is our God.

Proper 8

Sunday between 26 June and 2 July

2 KINGS 2:1–2, 6–14; PSALM 77:1–2, 11–20; GALATIANS 5:1, 13–25; LUKE 9:51–62

Opening prayer

Father, Son and Holy Spirit,
within whose unity
lies all that is God—
perfect love,
justice, peace
and power—
as we gather here today,
your body, your church
throughout this world,
fill our outstretched hearts
with your Spirit;
encircle us with your love;
make yourself known to us
in new ways,
exciting ways,
challenging ways.
Empower us;
inspire us,
glorious Trinity.

Adoration

In times of weakness and hour
    of need,
yours is the strength by which
    we carry on,
the shoulder we rest our
    head upon.
When the load is heavy and
    too much to bear,
yours is the strength that we
    can rely on,
the grace upon which we
    depend.
In times of weakness and hour
    of need,
your voice is heard:
'Come… find rest.'

This is grace divine,
the path we tread to wholeness
of body, mind and soul,
the path that leads to you,
for which we make this,
our offering of praise.

Confession

Father God,
you are the one who leads us
from darkness into light,
from captivity into freedom,
from anxiety into peace,
from despair into joy.
Yet we long to break free,
choosing independence,
convinced of our own wisdom,
forgetful of your love and
  grace.

Forgive our rebelliousness,
embrace us once again
in your loving arms
and enable us to follow you
in worship and grateful service
this and every day.

Thanksgiving

For the fruit of your Spirit,
wherever it is shown,
we give our grateful thanks.
For kindness shown by
  stranger
and faithfulness of friends,
for patience and forbearance
and peace that calms the soul,
for love that sees beyond the
  face
to the spirit deep within;
for the fruit of your Spirit,
wherever it is shown,
we give our grateful thanks.

Proper 9

Sunday between 3 and 9 July

2 KINGS 5:1–14; PSALM 30; GALATIANS 6:[1–6] 7–16; LUKE 10:1–11, 16–20

Opening prayer

In the meeting of our lives
be the unity that binds us.
In the opening of our hearts
be the mercy that forgives us.
In the speaking of our prayers
be the comfort that restores us.
In the singing of our hymns
be the joy we share between us.
In the journey of our lives
be the guiding light beside us.

Adoration

This world would deny you
and rely on human wisdom
in its search for answers,
but we will praise you
and exalt your name,
for we know that you are
   Alpha,
the beginning of all things,
and Omega,
the end of all things,
and everything between.

We have known your healing.
We have known your
   provision.
We have known your victory.
Our sorrow has turned into
   dancing
and our tears to songs of joy.
You are the answer
to all who need to know,
and we shall bring to you
   our praise.

Confession

For missed opportunities,
forgive us.
For hasty words and voices
  raised,
forgive us.
For selfishness and all that
  hurts,
forgive us.
For ears that fail to hear your
  word,
forgive us.
For eyes that look the other
  way,
forgive us.
For missed opportunities,
forgive us,
  revive us,
    restore us.

Teach us your way,
that we might walk in it
and be a blessing to all we meet
today and every day.

Thanksgiving

In your kingdom
there are no favourites,
for all are equal in your eyes,
marked with the image
of the one who formed
  creation,
moulded from the clay
from which all things are
  made.

In your kingdom of equality
you offer mercy to all
who, in humility,
come searching for your grace.
Such love,
beyond our imagining.
Such love,
that could die for us.
Such love,
sown into our hearts,
that we might display its
  beauty
through lives and words.
Thank you, Lord!

Year C

Proper 10

Sunday between 10 and 16 July

AMOS 7:7–17; PSALM 82; COLOSSIANS 1:1–14; LUKE 10:25–37

Opening prayer

Through our hymns and songs,
our prayer and meditation
and the joining of our lives,
we worship you,
Father, Son and Holy Spirit.
Enfold us in your love
and empower our worship,
that your name might be
  glorified
in this place and through our
  lives.

Adoration

You chose the very least of us
to be your prophets;
touched their lips
so they could speak your word;
protected them
when they faced opposition;
empowered them for service.

That you could entrust
  so much
to ordinary people
amazes us.
That you might entrust
  so much
to this, your church,
challenges us.
Amazing God,
be the strength that we desire,
the power within our lives,
that we might become the
  people
that you challenge us to be.

Confession

You call us to live your life,
to follow where you tread,
be your presence in our streets,
show compassion to the poor,
support the weak,
embrace the outcast
and bring the wanderers into
    your kingdom.
Yet our hearts are troubled;
we are fearful of the task,
deafened to your promise
to be with us
wherever we go.

Forgive our timidity;
grant us peace for the journey
and strength for our tasks,
that we might demonstrate
    your love
as we live and work day by
    day.

Thanksgiving

You call us to love those
whom you would love,
and you give us the words
    to say.
You call us to bring wholeness
to lives that are broken,
and you give us the words
    to say.
You call us to bring comfort
to those who are grieving,
and you give us the words
    to say.
You call us to bring good news
to those who are seeking,
and you give us the words
    to say.

We give thanks for your word,
    living water in desert sands;
your word,
    blossoming in parched earth;
your word,
    bearing fruit where it is sown.

Year C

Proper 11

Sunday between 17 and 23 July

AMOS 8:1–12; PSALM 52; COLOSSIANS 1:15–28; LUKE 10:38–42

Opening prayer

Eternal Father, be the love that
  dwells between us.
Healing Christ, be the peace
  that dwells between us.
Gracious Spirit, be the joy that
  dwells between us
in our times of worship and in
  our daily lives.

Adoration

Creator God,
from the moment your Spirit
hovered over the waters of this
  earth,
we were part of a vision
held lovingly within your
  heart.
From the moment you spoke
and separated darkness from
  light,
you created space
where we might one day walk.
From the moment your joy
spilled out into green and
  living things,
your beauty was revealed
for us to taste and see.

Creator God,
for this world,
beauty and majesty,
passion and artistry,
a green and pleasant place,
we praise your mighty name.

Confession

Remind us always of the
  path
we have chosen,
the one in whose footsteps
  we follow
and the service we offer.
When we are burdened
by the busyness of the day,
or tempted to wander
from our obedience to you,
forgive us.

Remind us always of your
  word
and draw us close,
that the concerns of this
  world
may fade into the hope
  that is to come.

Thanksgiving

Thank you for all who speak of you
through their word and lives,
your saints on earth
to whom we owe our knowledge
of your saving grace.

Leader: Wherever the seed of your
  love is sown
All: May it flourish and blossom.

Thank you for all who pray for us
through good times and bad,
your prayer warriors
who look at the bigger picture
with patience and hope.

Leader: Wherever the seed of your
  love is sown
All: May it flourish and blossom.

Thank you for all who serve you
in their everyday lives,
your loving saints
who bring your healing and
  comfort
wherever there is need.

Leader: Wherever the seed of your
  love is sown
All: May it flourish and blossom.

Year C

Proper 12

Sunday between 24 and 30 July

HOSEA 1:2–10; PSALM 85; COLOSSIANS 2:6–15 [16–19]; LUKE 11:1–13

Opening prayer

The blessing of Father, Spirit,
  Son,
Holy Trinity, three in one,
be in our meeting
and our greeting,
in the worship we share
and the words we pray.

The blessing of Father, Spirit,
  Son,
Holy Trinity, three in one,
be in our living
and our breathing,
that through our hearts and
  our lives
God's word may be heard.

Adoration

We do not follow idols
or earthly philosophies,
or place our hopes
in creeds devised by human
  minds.
Though we are small
when measured in universal
  terms,
and often powerless
when faced with difficulties
  or fear,
our hope is not founded
on the sand of the shore
but on the firm foundation
  of faith.

For we are children of a
  living God.
In him alone do we put our
  trust.
In him alone do we place our
  hope.
To him alone do we give our
  lives
to be used for his glory.

Confession

Gracious God,
whose love is greater
than the wickedness of this
  world,
forgive our wrongdoing.
Remind us of your love
and our indifference;
remind us of your peace
and our impatience;
remind us of your touch
and our brokenness;
remind us of your kingdom,
and our homelessness.

Gracious God,
whose love is greater
than the wickedness of this
  world,
draw us into your arms
and set our feet once more on
  solid ground.

Thanksgiving

Thank you, Lord,
that in your kingdom
there are no haves or
  have-nots,
no privileged or paupers,
no rich or exploited,
for in your eyes
all are of equal worth;
loved as only you can love,
blessed as only you can bless.

Thank you that we are
  counted as your children
and can open our hearts to a
  heavenly Father
who will listen to our prayer.
Thank you that we are
  precious in your sight,
and may our lives be counted
worthy of such love and grace.

Through Jesus Christ we ask,
who died that we might live,
and lives that we might
  know
the fullness of your love

Proper 13

Sunday between 31 July and 6 August

HOSEA 11:1–11; PSALM 107:1–9, 43; COLOSSIANS 3:1–11; LUKE 12:13–21

Opening prayer

Father of all,
we gather as your children
in fellowship together
 with you.

Saviour of all,
we gather to celebrate
the love which has its origins
 in you.

Spirit of all,
we gather in expectancy
with hearts open to receive
 from you.

Glorious Trinity,
we gather in worship
to proclaim the faith we have
 in you.

Adoration

Give thanks to the Lord, for he
 is good;
his love is inclusive,
embracing all creation!
Give thanks to the Lord, for he
 is good,
bringing wholeness,
and peace beyond
 understanding.
Give thanks to the Lord, for he
 is good,
his arms open wide,
welcoming prodigals home.
Give thanks to the Lord, for he
 is good,
his promises sure,
his kingdom everlasting.
Give thanks to the Lord, for he
 is good.

Confession

Loving God,
so often our lives
do not reflect the love
that you have shown us,
and in that we have failed you.
We ask for your mercy
and forgiveness.
We are blind
to injustices that we see,
and deaf
to voices crying out in need.
We follow our own path
through life, and choose
to ignore the one
that you would have us use,
fearing vulnerability.

Take our lives, dear Lord,
restore to us the love
that we once knew,
and let it pour from our hearts
into this world,
becoming a blessing
that we freely share.

Thanksgiving

We come now, Lord,
with grateful thanks,
for we can turn to you
when all is brokenness
and despair,
when answers
seem so insincere
and faith is struggling
to stay alive.

We can turn to you,
the one who knows
  the sadness of rejection
and the pain of sacrifice.
We can turn to you,
the one who knows
  the joy of resurrection
and brings us promise
of new life.
We can turn to you
and find peace
and comfort for our souls.

Thank you, Lord.

Proper 14

Sunday between 7 and 13 August

ISAIAH 1:1, 10–20; PSALM 50:1–8, 22–23; HEBREWS 11:1–3, 8–16; LUKE 12:32–40

Opening prayer

Bless the worship we present
  to you,
bless the hymns we sing
  to you,
bless us in our offering,
bless us in our coming,
bless us in our going,
and make our lives a blessing
on the road we travel.

Adoration

The heavens proclaim your
  glory
through creation's glorious
  song,
and all that live upon the earth
are moved to sing with them,
praising your gracious
  provision
and the glorious kingdom
established for your children,
revealed through your Son,
where we gain a foretaste
of the life that is to come.
Creator, Redeemer, Lord and
  King,
the heavens proclaim your
  glory
and we join them in their
  song.

Confession

God of love,
when your children suffer—
displaced,
persecuted or worse—
your heart is saddened
and you cry out for justice.
When apathy dulls our hearts
and we do not speak out,
forgive us.
When we are slow to respond
and somewhere lives are lost,
forgive us.
Give us a heart for justice
and a prophetic voice,
that this world might see
your love in action
through our words and deeds.

Thanksgiving

For faith to see through
  the mist
of our temporary problems
and glimpse the life beyond,
we give you thanks.

For faith to understand
  the reason
behind conflicts we encounter,
and wisdom to put them right,
we give you thanks.

For faith under persecution
  from those
who would deny the one we
  serve,
and strength to carry on,
we give you thanks.

For faith to claim your
  promises,
embrace them with our hearts
and express them in our lives,
we give you thanks.

Proper 15

Sunday between 14 and 20 August

ISAIAH 5:1–7; PSALM 80:1–2, 8–19; HEBREWS 11:29—12:2; LUKE 12:49–56

Opening prayer

We gather as your children,
forgiven and accepted,
meeting in this sacred place.
We gather as brother and
  sister,
family together,
meeting in our Father's house.
We gather as your body,
blessing each other
as the community of Christ.

Adoration

For the majesty of creation,
the heavens above
and the oceans below,
accept our offering of praise.

For the beauty of your love,
the wisdom, joy
and patience shown us,
accept our offering of praise.

For the sadness we cause you,
and your willingness
to forgive us,
accept our offering of praise.

For the knowledge of
  salvation,
Jesus' sacrifice
bringing life to us,
accept our offering of praise.

Confession

You have given us
a world of beauty,
and we have spoilt it.
A world to feed us,
and so many go hungry.
A world of riches,
and we are unwilling to share.
A world to care for,
and we think only of ourselves.

Forgive us, gracious God,
every time your heart is
  saddened
by our selfishness;
every time we have no
  thought
for others, no cares but our
  own.
Enable us to see this world
as a gift from you
that can be shared,
and those who live on it
as our neighbours.
We ask this, that your name
may be glorified
through the beauty and
  bounty of this world
and the service of our lives.

Thanksgiving

Faith is the gift
by which we see
this world through your eyes,
and the beauty that's within it.

Faith is the gift
by which we see
your image in all people,
and your blessing, if we
  receive it.

Faith is the gift
by which we see
the hope within your promise
and the strength by which to
  live it.

Faith is the gift
that is ever constant,
and we receive it
with grateful thanks.

Proper 16

Sunday between 21 and 27 August

JEREMIAH 1:4–10; PSALM 71:1–6; HEBREWS 12:18–29; LUKE 13:10–17

Opening prayer

God of the past,
accept the people we have been
and the baggage we drag
  behind us.

God of the present,
accept the people we are now,
with the concerns of this
  present moment.

God of the future,
accept the people we will be
and, by your Spirit,
  transform us.

Adoration

For the love you have
  shown us
since the moment we were
  born,
and the path you open for us
as your servants here on earth;
for the footsteps we follow,
and the words that we
  shall speak—
the seed that we scatter
as we walk your narrow way;
for the harvest you shall gather
on that great and glorious day,
O Lord, to you we offer
a sacrifice of praise.

Confession

Loving Father,
we are troubled
by those lost opportunities
when we failed to share your
  love,
held our tongue or turned
  away
from injustice or need.
Forgive us, we pray,
and by your Spirit
open our eyes
to daily possibilities
where we might serve you
and be your words and hands
in this, your beautiful
but fragile world.

Thanksgiving

For those moments when,
faced by difficult
  circumstances,
we are given a word
that calms a troubled soul,
or a gift of healing,
comfort or compassion
that has its source in you,
we offer our thanksgiving
  prayer.

For those moments when,
beset by doubt and uncertainty,
we are granted a faith
that sees beyond the present
to a future that is glorious,
and humility to accept the help
that comes through others
but ultimately from you,
we offer our thanksgiving
  prayer.

Proper 17

Sunday between 28 August and 3 September

JEREMIAH 2:4–13; PSALM 81:1, 10–16; HEBREWS 13:1–8, 15–16; LUKE 14:1, 7–14

Opening prayer

Creator of all,
we bring our offering of
  worship
for all that you have made
  for us.

Saviour of all,
we bring our offering of
  worship
for all that you have done
  for us.

Spirit of all,
we bring our offering of
  worship
for all that you reveal to us.

Three in one,
we bring our offering of
  worship;
be the blessing among us now.

Adoration

You are a faithful God,
when so often we fail you.
You are a forgiving God,
even when we deny you.
You are a patient God
when we stray far from you.
You are a welcoming God
as we come home to you.

Faithful and loving God,
accept the praises that we
  bring,
the offering of our hearts
and the service of our lives,
that we might faithfully
show your love
wherever we might go,
as together we continue
on our journey with you.

Confession

You call us
and we ignore your whisper,
listening instead to the voices
  of others.
You call us
and we choose a different path,
following our own devices.
You call us
to be your voice in this world,
to be your hands in this world,
to be your feet in this world,
to proclaim your peace,
your comfort,
forgiveness,
healing,
love
and grace.

Forgive us;
open our ears;
call us again
and we shall follow.

Thanksgiving

Thank you for the privilege of
  serving,
of sharing your love
through word and deed.
Thank you for the joy of
  knowing
that what we say
can bring such peace.
Thank you for the blessing of
  seeing
hearts touched
by the riches of your grace.

What a harvest there can be
when seeds we sow
produce fruitfulness!

Year C

Proper 18

Sunday between 4 and 10 September

JEREMIAH 18:1–11; PSALM 139:1–6, 13–18; PHILEMON 1–21; LUKE 14:25–33

Opening prayer

Lord God,
word and breath of life,
the peace between us,
the power among us.
Be in our singing,
in our praying,
in our coming and going.
Be the blessing we receive and
  share,
today and every day.

Adoration

Like clay in the potter's hand,
so we are to you, O Lord.
You take the ordinary
and imperfect,
making something beautiful,
moulding us into the people
you envisaged us to be.
In your hands we are made
  new,
perfected, Lord, by you.
In your hands we are made
  useful
in service, Lord, for you.

Confession

You know us, Lord,
better than we know
  ourselves.
You know our thoughts,
the unspoken prayers within
  our hearts.
You know our words
before they are formed on our
  tongues.
You know our lives,
our going out and coming
  home again.
You know us, Lord,
better than we know
  ourselves.

Forgive us when we fail to see
your wonder and majesty.
Open our eyes;
enlarge our faith,
that our knowledge of you
and our service to you
might increase
day by day.

Thanksgiving

God of the journey, we give
  you thanks.
You are the compass
  guiding us,
the light for our feet,
the one we follow.
You are the encouraging word,
the hand reaching for us
each time we stumble.

In our daily journeying
may we appreciate
the places you take us,
and, in word and action,
become a blessing
to our fellow travellers.
God of the journey,
we give you thanks.

Proper 19

Sunday between 11 and 17 September

JEREMIAH 4:11–12, 22–28; PSALM 14; 1 TIMOTHY 1:12–17; LUKE 15:1–10

Opening prayer

As we gather for worship,
let us pause a while in
  quietness,
stilling our hearts.
(Pause)

May the Lord be with us
in our singing,
the prayers we offer
and our understanding of
  scripture.
May our thoughts be on others
rather than self,
and our hearts stirred to
  service
wherever we might be.

Adoration

Son of God,
you love each one of us
as if there *were* just one of us.
Some have striven hard
to obey your commands;
some have found their way
after a journey that was long;
some have drifted here,
unsure of the path they trod;
some are here
simply because of your mercy
  and grace.

Son of God,
you love each one of us
as if there *were* just one of us.
How can we not sing your
  praises
for all that you have done?

Confession

Lord, we would follow you
wherever you might lead.
Lord, we would follow you.

Forgive us when we stray
and when we stumble.
Forgive us when we are
  sidetracked
and lose our way.
Be the one to whom we turn,
whose hand we hold,
the shepherd who leads us
safely home.

Lord, we would follow you
wherever you might lead.
Lord, we would follow you.

Thanksgiving

Gracious Father,
loving unconditionally,
whose heart
overflows with forgiveness,
this is our offering of thanks
  and praise.

Gracious Son,
giving sacrificially,
whose body
bled for our salvation,
this is our offering of thanks
  and praise.

Gracious Spirit,
flowing eternally,
whose breath
revives our faith and soul,
this is our offering of thanks
  and praise.

Year C

Proper 20

Sunday between 18 and 24 September
JEREMIAH 8:18—9:1; PSALM 79:1–9; 1 TIMOTHY 2:1–7; LUKE 16:1–13

Opening prayer
God of today and all days,
be with us as we meet—
the love that binds us,
the peace that calms us,
the touch that heals us,
the joy that fills us,
the arms that hold us.
Be with us as we meet,
God of today and all days.

Adoration
In a world that has so much
  to say
and no time for listening,
you love to hear your people's
  prayers,
that sweet and fragrant
  offering
rising upward to your throne.

In a world that asks so many
  questions
in its search for meaning,
you are the answer they seek,
living water that quenches
  thirst,
creator and source of all.

In a world that is searching
  for love
and a sense of purpose,
you welcome your prodigal
  children back
into a Father's loving arms
and to your family home.

Confession

If our neighbour does not
  know your name
because you have not been
  introduced,
forgive us.
If a friend or colleague is still
  searching
for the answers we already
  know,
forgive us.
If this world has yet to see
  the change
that lies hidden in our hearts,
forgive us.
If we have yet to find the
  courage
to talk about our faith,
forgive us,
  revive us,
and empower us to become
the disciples we ought to be,
that your name may be
  glorified
as it ought to be.

Thanksgiving

There is only one God,
who made all things
and creates within us
the image of the divine.

Leader: Good news to all
All: We proclaim with thanks.

There is only one Christ,
who died for us,
rose to life again
and now intercedes for us.

Leader: Good news to all
All: We proclaim with thanks.

There is only one Spirit,
who lives in us,
inspires our thoughts
and warms our hearts for
  service.

Leader: Good news to all
All: We proclaim with thanks.

God the Father, Spirit, Son,
glorious Trinity, three in one.

Leader: Good news to all
All: We proclaim with thanks.

Year C

Proper 21

Sunday between 25 September and 1 October

JEREMIAH 32:1–3A, 6–15; PSALM 91:1–6, 14–16; 1 TIMOTHY 6:6–19; LUKE 16:19–31

Opening prayer

Gracious God,
you know our needs,
read our thoughts,
see into our hearts
and yet accept us as we are.
Be the centre of our worship,
the focus of our prayer
and the one to whom we turn
as we meet today.

Adoration

God our fortress,
protection through storm and
    trouble,
strength when courage fails,
accept our offering of praise.

God our Saviour,
deliverer from the life that
    snares us,
the forgiveness that we seek,
accept our offering of praise.

God our refuge,
foundation on which we
    depend,
blessing that we now share,
accept our offering of praise.

Confession

The blessings of each day—
food to eat,
clothes to wear,
contentment with all we have,
whether rich or poor—
this is life in your kingdom.

How difficult it is
to walk along this road
when the world tempts us
with so much that we desire
but do not need.
Forgive our weakness
and teach us again
to know the contentment
of having just enough
and of sharing
not only from our riches
but from our poverty.

Thanksgiving

For all who have gone before,
walked the path we tread
and, by their example,
encouragement,
wise words and teaching,
have led others into your
  kingdom,
we offer our grateful thanks.

For all who, through their
  actions,
put others before self,
demonstrating the meaning
of generosity and love,
giving from their riches
and from their poverty,
we offer our grateful thanks.

We pray in the name of the
  one who gave
everything, that we might
understand the true
value of this life
and gain the riches
of the one to come,
Jesus Christ, our Lord.

Proper 22

Sunday between 2 and 8 October

LAMENTATIONS 1:1–6; PSALM 37:1–9; 2 TIMOTHY 1:1–14; LUKE 17:5–10

Opening prayer

May God, who brought us to
   this place,
accept the hymns and words
   we say here,
and may the love that joins us
   in his grace
be our blessing throughout
   the day.

Adoration

In you, O Lord, do we trust;
in your love we delight,
for there is no other
to whom we can turn,
who knows our needs
before we ask,
reads our hearts
and answers our requests.

In you, O Lord, do we trust;
in your peace we depend,
for there is no other
to whom we can turn,
who calms our souls,
brings release,
and, when we are weary,
in whose arms we rest.

Confession

Lord, we bring to you our
  'almost' moments.
When the opportunity arose to
  bring your name
into a conversation and we
  almost did.
When we were challenged to
  help someone in need, and
  almost did.
When we were angered by
  an injustice and, fired up to
  make a change, almost did.
When we heard your call
  to take a different path,
  and almost did.

Forgive our timidity, our
  reluctance
to live the life that we
  proclaim.
We bring to you our 'almost'
  moments.
By your Spirit empower our
  lives,
that your name might be
  glorified
and our 'almost' become
  'always'.

Thanksgiving

For the gift of faith,
which sees beyond the present
  moment
and looks to your eternity,
we thank you.

For the gift of faith,
small as a mustard seed,
  but with such strength
within that simplicity,
we thank you.

For the gift of faith,
bestowed on all those who
  simply ask,
their hearts open in humility,
we thank you.

Proper 23

Sunday between 9 and 15 October

JEREMIAH 29:1, 4–7; PSALM 66:1–12; 2 TIMOTHY 2:8–15; LUKE 17:11–19

Opening prayer

At this meeting of our lives,
may the love that is shown,
the concerns expressed,
the worship offered
and fellowship shared
be acceptable to you,
our heavenly Father.

Adoration

Praise the Lord, all people!
May our praises resound
  throughout the world!

Creator of the universe,
whose breath gives life,
whose hands create beauty,
whose love brings freedom,
whose glory fills the earth,
accept this offering of praise.

Saviour of the world,
whose touch gives healing,
whose words bring forgiveness,
whose suffering offers life,
whose death is victory,
accept this offering of praise.

Praise the Lord, all people!
May our praises resound
  throughout the world!

Confession

God of grace, we bring to you
our ingratitude
for all that you have done
  for us;
our impatience
when answers to prayer are
  delayed;
our selfishness
when prompted to give or
  share;
our unfaithfulness
when wandering from
  your way.
We ask for your forgiveness,
through Jesus Christ
who gave all
that we might learn to do
  likewise.
By your Spirit,
may our lives become more
  fruitful
and our hearts reflect nothing
  but you.

Thanksgiving

Thank you, Lord God,
for you call us to be
your light
in the darkness;
your voice
in the wilderness;
your hope
for the hopeless.

Thank you, Lord God,
for you give us
strength
in our weakness;
peace
and gentleness;
words
and boldness,
to proclaim
more of you
and, of us, less.

Proper 24

Sunday between 16 and 22 October

JEREMIAH 31:27–34; PSALM 119:97–104; 2 TIMOTHY 3:14—4:5; LUKE 18:1–8

Opening prayer

May our ears be attuned
to the whisper of God,
our hearts open
to the love of God,
our voices raised
in the worship of God
and our lives transformed
by the power of God.

Adoration

Your word is a lamp to
  our feet,
our guide through the dark,
the wisdom and knowledge
we follow each day.

Your word is sweeter than
  honey,
yet sharper than swords;
it is healing and justice
and ours to obey.

Your word is our
  understanding
of grace, peace and love—
the reason we gather
in worship today.

Confession

Saviour to all,
who healed the sick
and brought wholeness,
compassion
  and peace
to lives that were broken;
who brought direction,
purpose
  and joy
to those who were seeking;
who brought forgiveness,
wisdom
  and grace
to those who were thirsting;
grant us faith enough
to trust your word,
seek your face,
follow your footsteps
and know you as Lord.

Thanksgiving

God of justice,
we give thanks that you listen
to the cry of those
suffering oppression or fear,
the forgotten and ignored
who will always be your
  children.
God of justice, your will be
  done.

God of the poor,
we give thanks that you listen
to the cry of those
suffering hunger,
street children and refugees
who have nowhere to call
  their home.
God of the poor, your will be
  done.

Your will be done
through aid workers and
  politicians,
fundraisers and donors.
Your will be done through us.

God of all,
we give thanks that you listen
to your people's prayers.

Year C

Proper 25

Sunday between 23 and 29 October

JOEL 2:23–32; PSALM 65; 2 TIMOTHY 4:6–8, 16–18; LUKE 18:9–14

Opening prayer

In your house
and in your presence,
we join together
as we meet, pray
and sing to you.
When, afterwards, we go our
   separate ways,
may we live our lives in service
in our workplaces,
neighbourhoods
and family groups,
that your love
might be seen and known
through our words and
   actions.

Adoration

To you, O Lord, we bring our
   praise
in springtime and in autumn
   rains,
for seed sown and harvest
   gathered,
the abundant blessings of your
   world.

To you, O Lord, we bring our
   praise
for the beauty that we see
   around:
sunlit skies, mountain stream,
the mysteries of this universe.

To you, O Lord, we bring our
   praise
for the understanding of your
   grace,
words preached, lives changed,
the glorious challenge of your
   word.

Confession

Gracious God, forgive us
for the wrong we have done,
and the good we have not
 done—
for those times
when our words,
actions or inactions
have not reflected the love
you show to us.
Forgive us when we stumble
 on the path
that we are travelling
 with you.

Restore us.
Walk beside us,
that in your presence
we might become your hands
reaching out in love,
and your voice
bringing healing and peace
wherever there is need,
to your praise and glory.

Thanksgiving

You are our hope
when all else fails,
that solid rock
firm and secure,
on which we can depend.

Leader: Receive the thankful
 offering
All: Of these hearts and lives.

You are the source
of all we know,
the word of life,
love, grace and peace,
worth dying to defend.

Leader: Receive the thankful
 offering
All: Of these hearts and lives.

You are our God
and we shall walk
the path you tread,
prepared to go
wherever you may send.

Leader: Receive the thankful
 offering
All: Of these hearts and lives.

Fourth Sunday before Advent

Sunday between 30 October and 5 November

HABAKKUK 1:1–4; 2:1–4; PSALM 119:137–144; 2 THESSALONIANS 1:1–4, 11–12;
LUKE 19:1–10

Opening prayer

Father, Son and Holy Spirit,
bless us in our gathering,
our speaking and listening,
our sharing and worship,
our giving and receiving,
our coming and going.

Adoration

Saviour God,
you came into this world
not as a leader of men,
but as a servant and friend.
You came into this world
not to seek out the good
but to gather the lost.
You came into this world
as a healer of bodies
and saviour of souls.
You came into this world
as Prince of Peace
and lover of all.
You came into this world
for people like us.

Confession

When we call out your name
in times of hardship
or in our despair
and fail to hear your voice
or see the answer we desire,
forgive our impatience.

When we pray for healing,
freedom from fear
or relief from evil's grasp,
and grow weary of the task
of continuing in prayer,
forgive our lack of faith.

Your ways are not ours,
but in all things you are God;
your love and justice
will always prevail.
In your time and in your way
you will answer all our
  prayers.

Thanksgiving

For all your servants
who have gone before
and, by their example,
have brought us to your
  throne,
we offer our grateful thanks.

For all who, through
dark days and nights,
held on to their faith
against the fiercest foe,
we offer our grateful thanks.

For all your children
gathered here today,
who, by their service,
show your love in this world,
we offer our grateful thanks.

Year C

All Saints Day

1 November or the first Sunday in November

DANIEL 7:1–3, 15–18; PSALM 149; EPHESIANS 1:11–23; LUKE 6:20–31

Opening prayer

Here we are,
your ordinary saints
worshipping their Maker.
Here we are,
your ordinary people,
by the power of your Spirit
experiencing the
  extraordinary;
your ordinary servants
living the truth of your word,
being your hands and voices in
  this world.

Adoration

Glorious Father, Lord of all,
we lift your name on high.
You reveal the blessings
of life in your kingdom,
giving us knowledge
of love and mercy;
drawing us closer
into your presence;
healing our brokenness;
tending our souls;
opening our lives to
your love and grace.
Glorious Father, Lord of all,
we lift your name on high.

Confession

Who are the poor
but those who know they have
  nothing
without you?
Who are the hungry
but those who know their
  sustenance comes
only from you?
Who are the sorrowful
but those who weep for the
  many
who don't know you?

Give us your heart
for those who are seeking;
give us your heart
for those who are suffering;
give us your heart
for those in this world
who, though they have
  nothing,
have all that they need
if they will but reach out
  for you.

Thanksgiving

The blessed in your eyes
are not those who have
  everything
but those who consider
that without you
they have nothing.
Not the rich in earning,
but the rich in spending,
who give their lives for you.
Your ordinary saints,
being your hands
and speaking your words
in their ordinary lives,
doing extraordinary things
with all that you have given
  them.

The blessed in your eyes
are not those who desire
  honour,
but those who seek to serve.
Thank you for the servants in
  your kingdom.

Year C

Third Sunday before Advent

Sunday between 6 and 12 November

HAGGAI 1:15B—2:9; PSALM 145:1–5, 17–21; 2 THESSALONIANS 2:1–5, 13–17;
LUKE 20:27–38

Opening prayer

God of love,
be the love that dwells in this
  place.

Prince of peace,
be the peace that dwells in this
  place.

Spirit of life,
be the life that dwells in this
  place.

Three in one,
be the everything in our
  emptiness,
the completeness in our
  imperfection,
all we desire.

Adoration

Leader: Great is the Lord
All: And most worthy of praise.

Saints who have gone before
speak of your glory,
their words passed down
as a living witness
to your love and grace.

Leader: Great is the Lord
All: And most worthy of praise.

Your love speaks more than
  words;
it fills our emptiness,
warms our spirits
and draws us once again
into your embrace.

Leader: Great is the Lord
All: And most worthy of praise.

Confession

In our hearts we know
that you are Lord
of this world and the next.
In our hearts we know
that you are truth:
all wisdom comes from you.
In our hearts we know
that you are love,
for this has touched our lives.

When we are swayed
by words that tempt
and keep us from your path,
forgive us, Lord, we pray.
Burnish our hearts,
so we reflect
only light that comes
  from you.

Thanksgiving

Spirit of God,
present with us,
living in us,
revealed through us:

Leader: Fill these lives
**All: With thanks overflowing
  to you.**

Spirit of truth,
wisdom and peace,
river of life
flowing through us:

Leader: Fill these lives
**All: With thanks overflowing
  to you.**

Spirit of grace,
gentle whisper
prompting us
to lives of service:

Leader: Fill these lives
**All: With thanks overflowing
  to you.**

Second Sunday before Advent

Sunday between 13 and 19 November

ISAIAH 65:17–25; PSALM 98; 2 THESSALONIANS 3:6–13; LUKE 21:5–19

Opening prayer

In this day of new beginnings
be the focus of our worship:
the Father who loves us,
the Son who hears us,
the Spirit within us,
the unity between us,
the life we live.

Adoration

In our journeying with you
there is a destination.
Some travel light,
unencumbered
by life's baggage,
hands free to serve
and help along the road.
Some travel slowly,
overburdened
by all they carry,
and needing some
assistance with their load.

So it is, as travellers,
we meet along the way,
and take, or lend a hand.
There is a destination
toward which we walk—
into your presence
where, with the angels,
we shall worship you each day.

Confession

Keep us close, we pray.
Be the one to whom we turn
when faced with fear,
uncertainty
and questioning.
Be the rock on which
  we stand,
the truth we hold to
and the certainty
to which we cling.
Be the Father in whose arms
we gladly fall,
the security
in our journeying.
Keep us close, we pray.

Thanksgiving

When we walk with you
in the light of your love,
it is your glory seen,
not ours.

When we talk of you
to those whom we meet,
it is your words that speak,
not ours.

When we minister
to people in need,
it is your hands that heal,
not ours.

Thank you, Lord God,
that when we worship you
and offer our lives,
your name is glorified
always.

Year C

Christ the King

Sunday between 20 and 26 November

JEREMIAH 23:1–6; PSALM 46; COLOSSIANS 1:11–20; LUKE 23:33–43

Opening prayer

Into your presence we come,
Saviour, Shepherd and King,
your servants
with our offering
of worship,
thanksgiving
and song.
Gifts from our riches
and gifts from our poverty.
Gifts to our Saviour, Shepherd
  and King.

Adoration

Before all things began,
  you were,
one with Father and Spirit
  in glorious unity.
Before all things began,
  you were,
our lives within your thoughts,
our future in your heart.

Before all things began,
  you were,
creation and redemption
perfected in your plan.
Before all things began,
  you were,
king and kingdom waiting,
for time is in your hands.

Confession

Shepherd-king,
who leads us to green pastures
and keeps us safe from harm,
you love each one of us
and know us all by name.

Forgive us when we
  wander away
and follow another's call;
forgive us when we try to
  hide from you,
afraid of what we are.
Forgive us and draw us back
into your loving arms,
and in your presence
  once more
we'll truly see your face.

Thanksgiving

The kingdom of God
is here among us,
where his children
walk freely
from all that once kept them
  enslaved.

The kingdom of God
is here among us,
where his justice
is made known
not by force but by an
  empty grave.

The kingdom of God
is here among us,
where his power
is revealed
in the lives of those who
  believe.

The kingdom of God
is here among us.
Receive the grateful thanks
of your people, Lord.

52 Reflections on Faith for Busy Preachers and Teachers

Stephen W. Need

These 52 reflections—one for each week of the year—provide short, sharp and profound insights into Christian faith and life. The aim is to stimulate thinking rather than provide all the answers, and show how faith can connect up with daily life, Bible teaching and also wider culture.

While the first half is based on themes of special relevance to Sundays throughout the Christian year, from Advent to the feast of Christ the King, the second half of the book considers core aspects of Christian belief, starting with God and ending with the risen Jesus on the Emmaus road. Offering a wealth of personal inspiration for preachers as well as stimulating material for group or individual study, the book makes an excellent ordination, commissioning or licensing gift.

ISBN 978 1 84101 743 3   UK £12.99
Available from your local Christian bookshop or direct from BRF:
please visit www.brfonline.org.uk

Also from BRF

Living Liturgies

Transition time resources for services, prayer and
conversation with older people

Caroline George

This book offers a creative worship resource for pastoral
ministry with those at an often overlooked time of life—the
move from independent living to dependency, or from the
'third age' to the 'fourth age' of life. The twelve liturgies—and
accompanying reflections for those leading the worship—were
developed by Caroline George after many years of working in
church and community settings with older people and provide
valuable help for those embarking on this ministry, as well as
inspiration for those already involved.

Each specially written liturgy uses a simple structure based
around a theme to weave together experience, scripture and
the assurance of God's love and grace. Conversation is used to
connect the theme with past, present and future, leading into
prayer and silent reflection with the help of a visual aid.

ISBN 978 0 85746 323 4   UK £7.99
Available January 2015 from your local Christian bookshop or direct
from BRF: please visit www.brfonline.org.uk

Creating a Life with God

The call of ancient prayer practices

Daniel Wolpert

Are you longing to take your relationship with God to a new level?

This book introduces you to twelve prayer practices that

- invite you to solitude and silence
- invite you to use your mind and imagination
- invite you to use your body and your creativity
- invite you to connect with nature and community

You'll meet 'travelling companions' from history, such as Ignatius Loyola and Julian of Norwich—individuals and groups whose lives were illuminated by these ways of praying. An appendix offers step-by-step instructions for practising the Jesus Prayer and the prayer of examen, for walking a labyrinth, praying with your body, and more—whether individually or as a group.

ISBN 978 0 85746 244 2   UK £7.99
Available from your local Christian bookshop or direct from BRF: please visit www.brfonline.org.uk

80 Creative Prayer Ideas

A resource for church and group use

Claire Daniel

Prayer is a vital part of the Christian life but people often struggle with actually getting on and doing it. This book offers 80 imaginative and creative ideas for setting up 'prayer stations', practical ways of praying that involve the senses—touching, tasting, smelling, seeing and hearing, rather than simply reflecting—as we bring our hopes, fears, dreams and doubts to God.

Developed from material tried and tested with small groups, the ideas provide activities ranging from bubble prayers to clay pot prayers (via just about everything else in between), and have been designed to be used with grown-ups of all ages.

ISBN 978 1 84101 688 7   UK £7.99
Available from your local Christian bookshop or direct from BRF: please visit www.brfonline.org.uk

Using the Jesus Prayer

Steps to a simpler Christian life

John Twisleton

In a hectic world, we so often struggle to find ways of growing in faith and, especially, deepening our experience of prayer. While many have been inspired by documentaries about contemplative prayer and monastic life, it remains a challenge to sustain disciplines of prayer and worship in the busyness of everyday life.

The Jesus Prayer of Eastern Orthodoxy, 'Lord Jesus Christ, Son of God, have mercy on me, a sinner', offers a simple yet profound way of developing such discipline. Thoroughly biblical, carried forward by the faith of the Church through the centuries, it stands as a unique gift and a task for us. In this book on the Jesus Prayer, its succinct summary of faith and its capacity to empower, John Twisleton gives practical guidance on how to use it, as well as exploring the simplicity of life it offers.

ISBN 978 1 84101 778 5   UK £6.99
Available from your local Christian bookshop or direct from BRF: please visit www.brfonline.org.uk

Enjoyed

this book?

Write a review—we'd love to hear what you think.
Email: reviews@brf.org.uk

Keep up to date—receive details of our new books as they happen.
Sign up for email news and select your interest groups at:
www.brfonline.org.uk/findoutmore/

Follow us on Twitter @brfonline

By post—to receive new title information by post (UK only), complete
the form below and post to: BRF Mailing Lists, 15 The Chambers, Vineyard,
Abingdon, Oxfordshire, OX14 3FE

Your Details
Name _____
Address _____
_____
Town/City _____ Post Code _____
Email _____

Your Interest Groups (*Please tick as appropriate)	
☐ Advent/Lent	☐ Messy Church
☐ Bible Reading & Study	☐ Pastoral
☐ Children's Books	☐ Prayer & Spirituality
☐ Discipleship	☐ Resources for Children's Church
☐ Leadership	☐ Resources for Schools

Support your local bookshop
Ask about their new title information schemes.